PROJECT

MANAGEMENT

for

TRAINERS

**STOP WINGING IT AND
GET CONTROL OF YOUR
TRAINING PROJECTS**

 **ASTD Press**

Lou Russell

Ordering information: Books published by ASTD can be ordered by calling 800.628.2783 or 703.683.8100, or via the Website at **store.astd.org.**

Library of Congress Catalog Card Number: 00-104277

ISBN: 1-56286-141-7

Printed by Victor Graphics, Inc. Baltimore, MD. www.victorgraphics.com

Project Management
for **Trainers**

Contents

Preface

Developing, implementing, and managing training projects requires sophisticated project management skills to bring a project to completion on time and within budget. Yet, many trainers either do not have those skills or apply the project approach they have developed in an inconsistent manner.

This book describes a project management approach and development process that I created to provide my company with a flexible structure to manage projects. This approach was born out of necessity and, in truth, developed in the school of hard knocks as I developed a successful consulting business, in which a repeatable approach to developing training programs is essential to success.

In the case of my business, the need for a solid project management approach to training development became evident as the projects of our growing company got larger and more complex. Often we were serving multiple clients with conflicting needs, changing business requirements, and a host of other uncertainties. These more complex projects required multiple developers to work together in a team, a new notion for a business that often relied on the individual, "seat of the pants" approach to developing and managing projects. Obviously, problems arose as personalities clashed and more and more hours were required to redo incompatible work created by other team members. Work was not delivered consistently, and our clients began to notice our struggles. It was time for some structure—not so much structure that flexibility was lost, but enough structure to improve the effectiveness of a company on the road to having some serious problems.

You may very well have your own structure, and it doesn't really matter whose you use, as long as you have one that works. What matters most is that the project is planned, organized, and controlled in a way that allows the needs of the customer to be met, regardless of how often they change or how many people are involved. Managing the project development is the key; it is precisely what allows any development approach to be both structured and flexible at the same time. It forces us to squarely keep our eyes on the customer's learning need rather than our snazzy methodology.

When creating courses, you may very well be able to "wing it," especially if you know the material well, you are going to teach it yourself, or the customer base is well defined. Unfortunately, this is not the way the business world is right now. Often, trainers are being asked to write courses that will be taught by others, maybe even by a computer or some other type of technology. We are being asked to develop course materials about things we know virtually nothing about and deliver them in a week. We are being asked to negotiate differences in requirements within the companies we are serving while negotiating the natural conflict and competition of our own development teams who must navigate this complexity. These are all project management problems.

Tighten *your* project management process before it is too late. Change the way you think about course development projects. Fight the urge to skip ahead to a solution, to visualize the exercises and content while your customer is describing his or her needs. The steps in this book will help you completely define a development project before you start planning the details of the development.

Expect each project to progress completely differently from your plan, and then forgive yourself when it does. A project done correctly is a project whose plan has adapted to the changing needs of the customer. If nothing happens that surprises you on a project, you probably did not add much value for the customer.

This particular project has had its surprises, but Mark Morrow at ASTD has been wonderful about allowing me the flexibility to meet the needs as they have changed. He has been a joy to work with—thank you, Mark. Since this is my second book, I had more of a process and more realistic expectations this time. My staff also knew exactly how to help me, especially LuAnn Woodruff, who did all the detail work that is such a struggle for me. Carol Mason and Margie Brown helped her, and as you are reading this, Vija Dixon is carefully implementing a comprehensive strategy for marketing this book to leverage our course development, project management teaching, and consulting services. She is a natural planner and provides a nice complement to my natural "do-er" personality.

Janice Daly, Pam Hager, and Jose Valencia will now find out that they were my researchers. They struggled together through a difficult development project while I was writing, and their stories helped me create many of the pointers and checklists you will read about here. They have provided many of the real-life, in-the-trenches nuggets that will be so valuable to you. In addition, they have shown great "servant leadership" (as defined by Robert Greenleaf—see the resource list) in their desire and effort to look back at this project and learn from it as a community of practice. The knowledge we have gained from this one project is going to push Russell Martin & Associates to the next level. Thank you Janice, Pam, and Jose for all your efforts.

Finally, thanks to my three little project managers, my daughters, Kelly, Kristin, and Katherine. Kelly is amazing at planning, organizing, and controlling her schoolwork and activities successfully. Kristin can plan a strategy that has the complexity many adults could not create. Katherine can think three steps ahead of where you are right now. I am proud to be their mom.

And to my husband, Doug, I owe the greatest thanks, of course. As a team, we have created a flexible structure to manage the complex balance of our lives. His devotion as both a husband and a father is most important to me and gives me the confidence to create.

It's time to begin your project. In chapter 1, you will read about how to get the most out of this book.

Lou Russell
October 2000

Chapter 1 —————————

Beginning the Project

Q: Why worry about project management in training areas?

A: Most of the work you do now is project work.

In this chapter, you will learn how to do the following:

- Differentiate between project management and learning event (course) development work

- Define the roles of the project manager, the project sponsor, and other key people in a learning project.

Whether it is developing a new course, adapting an existing course, finding the right self-paced solution, rolling out the right training administration program, or hiring the right external supplier, you are constantly working on projects. It would be important to know project management if you were working on a single project full time. It is vital to know how to manage projects when you are working on multiple, complex projects, as today's workload demands.

In this book, you will learn practical, not academic, techniques for rolling out customer solutions. A business problem in your or your client's organization will generally drive your project work. This business problem will be caused by either a missing skill (something people can't do), a missing piece of knowledge (something people don't know), or an inappropriate attitude (something people believe) that is hurting performance. The solution to this business problem may take many forms at implementation. Some type of training intervention may be part of the solution, but it is rarely the only piece needed. The training element may take the form of instructor-led, computer-based, video-based, Web-based, teleconferenced, or even paper tutorials—all of which are referred to in this book as *learning events*. Other solution components may take the form of a formalized mentoring procedure, a facilitated problem-solving session, or study group. These interventions fall into the category of *performance consulting*. In all these cases, project management will be required to define, plan, manage, and review the solution to ensure the right business results.

What Is a Project?

The best place to start is to clearly define what you mean by *project*. It may seem obvious, but it often isn't. A project has a distinct beginning and end. For example, developing a new course is a project. You start it on a particular day, and on another day, the course is implemented and someone learns from it (you hope). Of course, an ongoing set of activities may maintain and enhance this course as it lives its useful life—those activities constitute a maintenance process, not a project. Ongoing activities without a specific end point are called *processes*. The lists below illustrate the differences between the two types of activities:

Project	Process
Creation of a one-day workshop	Mentoring an employee
Creation of a Web-based training registration system	Administration of training activities
Creation of a compensation plan	Performance review
An organizational needs analysis	Negotiating a contract

Notice that processes can be redesigned and even removed; although they are important to the business, they don't really end. They are clocks that keep running until their usefulness wears out. A project, in contrast, would be the initial building of the clock.

What Is Project Management?

At a recent training session, one learner was overheard to say, "I just came out of development work to be a project manager." This is a refreshing statement, because not only do people confuse process and projects, they also confuse development and project work. The cost of this confusion is that people neglect project management work, which causes development to continue without a direction or plan, leading to missed deadlines, poor quality, or expensive rework.

Simply put, project management consists of *planning, organizing,* and *controlling* work. The person responsible for project management plans for the needs of a project, then organizes and controls project resources as the project progresses. This person has one foot in the future (creating a plan), one foot in the past (learning from mistakes), and the rest of the body in the present (reacting to surprises). This role is that of the project manager.

Project development work, for example, takes place when learning events are being constructed. When done correctly, it involves analysis of a skills or knowledge gap, design of the solution, and the building and testing of this solution. On large course-development projects, different people with different skill sets may get involved along the way. A person who is excellent at analyzing these gaps generally is not as skilled at design, a truism that highlights the need to differentiate between project management and development activities. Below are some examples of project management and project development activities:

Project Management Activity	Project Development Activity
Creating a project schedule	Writing learning objectives
Holding a status meeting	Constructing a prototype unit
Hiring more resources	Testing a computer-based tutorial

The project manager has a broad perspective; he or she watches the entire forest, not a specific tree. That is why it is so difficult to be the project manager and the course developer at the same time. The project manager keeps track of the gap between planned and actual time, cost, scope, and quality (more on this in chapter 2). The course developer, in contrast, focuses on creating the actual learning event. Each role has a specific, distinct focus. In learning-organization lingo, the project manager and the course developer do *not* have a "shared vision of priorities."

You may find that you have to play the role of both the developer and the project manager. When that is the case, consider blocking time for project management on your calendar to ensure that it gets done. Development is more easily measured and may tempt you away from project management time.

With today's workload, it is not uncommon for people to have to play many roles—and play them in half the time that is needed. This situation makes having control of project management even more important. Someone has to see the problems coming and react before the project is torpedoed. As projects become more complex and risky, project management is the only way to hedge your bets toward success.

Important Stakeholder Roles

The stakeholders also can make or break a project; they hold the keys to success. Because they ultimately will be the judge of project success, the project manager must constantly manage the communications with the stakeholders to ensure that their expectations are appropriate. Some stakeholder roles are listed below:

- **Return-on-Investment.** The *budget client* is the person who controls the money. He or she may not be the same person who requested the learning project, but the budget client will be the person who pays for it. Ask your contact whose signature you will need for your purchases, and you will find out who the budget client is. This client has the power to cancel the project at any time; he or she is accountable for the cost of the project and how it will provide a return to the business. Discussions about quality and time, unless directly related to dollars, will usually not be as meaningful as discussions about money.

- **Needs Analysis.** The *business client* is the person who has requested the project or a subject matter expert. For example, a manager having trouble with an employee might request that you develop a one-day leadership workshop for her entire staff. In many situations, business clients think they know what they want but may be unclear about what they need—or rather, what the business needs. Many times, business clients will come to you with a wrong or incomplete solution, and it is the project managers' and the developers' joint responsibility to facilitate thinking about what the business problems and the true needs actually are. Tools for this task will be explored in more detail in the following chapters.

- **Performance.** *Learners* are the people who have the gaps in skills, knowledge, or attitude. They may (or may not) be conscious of this gap. Learners will be the first people to evaluate the quality of the learning delivered and will provide feedback through words or behavior to the business and budget clients. If the project manager and developer get input from learners throughout the development project, the results will be better aligned to the business need.

Navigating This Book

Having spent some time now contrasting project management and development work and defining some roles, you may be thinking that the differences are not always clear-cut—and you're right. Naturally, there are places where the lines get pretty muddy. To be effective at managing learning projects, you must be able to plan, organize, and control, but you also must be clear which activities others will own. Performing these activities is development work, but scheduling, tracking, adjusting, and watching the activities is the core responsibility of the project manager. For that reason, this book will focus on both project management techniques and development activities.

This book is structured around an approach called The Dare Approach (see figure 1.1). Using the mnemonic "Dare to Properly Manage Resources," this book will introduce you to the phases called *define, plan, manage,* and *review* (which correspond to the first letters of each of the words in the phrase). An overview of how the chapters relate to these phases follows.

Chapter 1: Beginning the Project. In this chapter, you have been reading about a definition for project management, the roles of the project team, and the responsibilities of the project manager. The language introduced in this chapter will help you understand the other chapters.

Chapter 2: Defining the Project. In the first phase of The Dare Approach (the define phase), you will learn how to build a project definition. This phase documents the project scope, the initial business and project objectives, the risks and constraints, and alternatives for solutions.

Chapter 3: Planning the Project. In the second phase of The Dare Approach (the plan phase), you will learn how to build a project plan by creating a work breakdown structure and a project schedule using the critical path method and Gantt charts. You also will learn how to estimate and assign resources to project activities. In addition, you will learn how to create the budget using a costing worksheet and create a stakeholder communication plan.

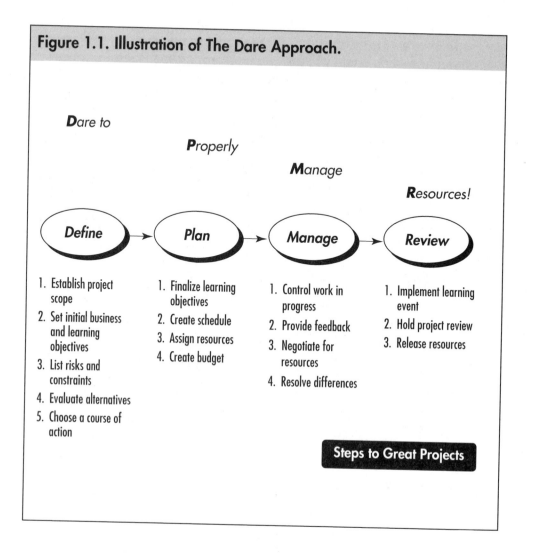

Figure 1.1. Illustration of The Dare Approach.

*D*are to

*P*roperly

*M*anage

*R*esources!

Define → **Plan** → **Manage** → **Review**

1. Establish project scope
2. Set initial business and learning objectives
3. List risks and constraints
4. Evaluate alternatives
5. Choose a course of action

1. Finalize learning objectives
2. Create schedule
3. Assign resources
4. Create budget

1. Control work in progress
2. Provide feedback
3. Negotiate for resources
4. Resolve differences

1. Implement learning event
2. Hold project review
3. Release resources

Steps to Great Projects

Chapter 4: A Course Development Template. A project manager sometimes needs a little help figuring out what activities need to be planned, organized, and controlled. In this chapter, you will learn about a development methodology called The Learner First Model. You will learn how to analyze a learning gap and then design and implement a solution. This solution also will leverage accelerated learning to ensure maximum retention.

Chapter 5: Managing the Project. Returning to the third phase of The Dare Approach (the manage phase), you will learn how to judge the status of a project by establishing and monitoring criteria, how to manage change, and what to do if you're behind.

Chapter 6: Reviewing the Project. In the fourth phase of The Dare Approach (the review phase), you will learn why looking back is so important to building project management skills and how you can apply a standard evaluation process to capture and share lessons learned.

Chapter 7: Managing Performance Consulting Projects. Managing the internal development of a new learning event is less difficult than the management of a performance consulting project. Because many training professionals are moving into performance consulting, it is essential to know how project management affects the success of these more complex projects. In this chapter, you will read about creating a rational plan for performance consulting. It is a realistic approach that works backward from the due date and is called The Pact Approach.

Chapter 8: A Template for Managing External Suppliers. Training projects often are outsourced to external providers. People vital to the project's success are required to manage mutually beneficial relationships with outside developers. In this chapter, you will learn about balancing detail and flexibility, managing contractor law, honoring confidentiality, establishing communication standards, managing change, negotiating effectively, and planning for knowledge transfer and shared risk.

Chapter 9: The Project Begins ... Chapter 9 will encourage you to make a personal commitment to improving your project management abilities on your projects.

Resources. This part of the book contains resources for you to continue building your own and your staff's skills in project management.

How to Take Advantage of This Book

The first step to successfully applying this book to your job is to set some goals for learning. Pick your most important learning objectives from table 1.1. Although it would be wonderful if you had the time to read this book from cover to cover, focus on the objectives most pertinent to you and your situation if you do not have that time.

Finally, think about a development project of any kind that you recently managed or are managing (for example, writing a new course, buying a new course, or hiring a supplier to teach a course). Throughout this book, starting with exercise 1.3, you will be asked to apply this experience to improve

Table 1.1. Learning objectives and corresponding chapters.

Learning Objective	Chapters
Accurately estimate work effort for a project	3, 4, 8
Adjust critical path networks and Gantt (bar) charts with actual status results to manage the project schedule and resource allocation	5
Build a project charter to document business objectives, learning objectives, scope, risks, and constraints	7, 8
Build a project plan for a new learning event development, course acquisition, or contracted training project	4, 8
Build a project plan for learning event course development	3
Build a stakeholder communication plan	2
Choose the appropriate activities for each project	4
Choose the appropriate activities to manage for a performance consulting effort	7
Create a work breakdown structure to uncover the activities needed to complete a project	3, 4, 8
Create critical path networks and Gantt charts as part of a project plan	3
Create critical path networks and Gantt charts to manage the project schedule and resource allocation	4, 8
Define the roles of the project manager, the project sponsor, and other key people in a learning project	1
Determine the tasks that need to be performed by the project manager and those that should be performed by a developer	3, 5, 7, 8
Differentiate between project management and development work	1
Document the business objectives of the learning event project	2
Document the learning objectives of the learning event	2
Document the risks and constraints of a learning event project	2
Document the scope of a learning event project	2
Estimate the cost of training projects	3
Evaluate alternatives and choose one	2
Finalize the business objectives of the learning project	3

Learning Objective	Chapters
Finalize the learning objectives of the learning event	3
Manage the cost of training projects	5
Monitor the project charter to document business objectives, learning objectives, scope, risks, and constraints	5
Monitor the project plan for new course development, course acquisition, or contracted training project	5
Perform a postproject review for every project to ensure the knowledge management of project intellectual capital	6, 8
Plan and manage the cost of training projects	4, 8

the project management for either a current or a future project of your own. (The book usually refers to this project as "your own project.") As you reflect on your project experiences, you will begin to see how important good project management is.

Summary

"The will to win is not nearly as important as the will to prepare to win." This quote, attributed to Indiana University basketball coach Bobby Knight, reflects my belief that effective project management results from the combination of a flexible, but repeatable, process and a growing, intelligent mind. This book will show you how to create that combination.

Practical Exercises

Exercise 1.1. Project management vs. development.

List the activities you worked on yesterday in the first column of the table provided.

Was each activity a project management activity or a development activity?

Place a check mark in the appropriate box. Write the amount of time you spent on each activity in the correct column.

Take a close look at what percentage of your time is development work and what percentage is project management work. Reflect on whether additional planning, organizing, and controlling could improve your project's success.

Project Activity	Management	Time Spent	Development	Time Spent
1.				
2.				
3.				
4.				
5.				

Exercise 1.2: Analysis.

Look at the table you created in exercise 1.1 and consider what happened on your last project.

Which of the factors contributing to the success of the project relate to project management (planning, organizing, and controlling)?

Which of the factors that contributed to problems relate to a lack of project management?

Take a few minutes and make some notes here for later reference.

What tasks helped you successfully complete your project?

What tasks—or tasks neglected—made your project more difficult?

_____

_____

_____

_____

_____

_____

_____

_____

_____

_____

_____

_____

_____

_____

_____

Exercise 1.3: Your own project.

Think about a development project of any kind that you recently managed or need to manage (for example, writing a new course, buying a new course, or hiring a supplier to teach a course). Answer the questions below and jot down some notes in the space provided.

What went well on the last project you managed?

What would you do differently on the next project?

What would you repeat? Consider deadlines, cost and budget factors, quality, scope, politics, change, and other factors.

Chapter 2 ────────────────────┐

Defining the Project

Q: Why do most projects struggle?

A: The scope of the project changes
without the resources changing.

This chapter will show you how to do the following:

- Document the scope of a learning event project
- Document the business objectives of the learning event project
- Document the learning objectives of the learning event
- Document the risks and constraints of a learning event project
- Evaluate alternatives and choose one
- Build a stakeholder communication plan.

When a project begins, or in order to get funding to begin, the project manager must create a *project charter.* This document can be called many different things (for example, the overall project plan, the project mission, or the scope document of understanding), but its role is the same: to clearly define the assumptions at the start of the project. The mission document should include material that covers

- the business objectives,
- the learning objectives,
- the scope,
- the risk,

- the constraints, and

- the stakeholder communication plan.

In this chapter, you will practice creating each of these elements.

Documenting the Business Objectives

Business objectives may seem obvious to the project manager and the developer, but they aren't always obvious to the stakeholders. In many ill-fated instances, projects proceed without any real business objectives, only to turn into workshops that are never attended or Web-based packages that are never installed. Everything that is done in a business should contribute to the goals of the business. In other words, unless there is business problem, there shouldn't be a solution.

Business objectives can be remembered easily with the mnemonic IRACIS, which represents the first letters in the phrases that capture the essence of business. No matter what project a business funds, everyone needs to be clear on how the project will

- increase revenue (IR),

- avoid cost (AC), and

- improve service (IS).

In some situations, project work is required to react to government regulation changes. For example, accountants need to be retrained in tax law changes. This learning may not as obviously meet the IRACIS criteria, although it does generally avoid the costs of fines or embarrassment. Likewise, many learning projects are geared toward creating a competitive advantage, such as salespeople who need to be retrained in the latest sales techniques. This learning won't guarantee increased revenue, but such retraining is a speculative investment that is based on that hope.

A Project Management Case to Think About

Below is a fictional case example that helps demonstrate the types of project deliverables that are expected of a successful project manager.

Although this book will be most useful for you if you keep in mind your own project (that is, the project that you thought of at the end of chapter 1), you will see references to this fictional case throughout the entire book.

Case Example Pretend that you have been asked to create a one-hour, instructor-led workshop on how to plan and hold a meeting. After talking with the business managers who have asked for this workshop, you find out that recent employee surveys have shown that the staff thinks that more than half the time they spend in meetings is wasted time. If that is true, it is costing the company huge amounts of money in lost productivity.

In addition, you learn that an organization has been hired to design a set of meeting guidelines that will be enforced at every meeting. If the guidelines aren't followed, people attending meetings have been instructed to leave. Your project will be to introduce the entire staff, through one-hour workshops, to those guidelines before the "leaving" approach is adopted.

While uncovering the business objectives, keep asking "why?" Why do you want a one-hour workshop on meetings? Why are employees unproductive in meetings? Why does this lack of productivity cost the business money? The more "why questions" you can ask, the better. In fact, most learning project managers stop asking these questions too soon.

Below is a list of the business objectives that the project manager might build and review with the stakeholders in the fictional case example presented above:

- By managing more effective use of meeting time, the company will avoid the labor cost of lost productivity. According to the employee survey, the average employee making $10 per hour who goes to one meeting a day for two hours loses $10 in labor productivity, because only 50 percent of the time spent in meetings is productive. (AC: avoid cost)

- By managing more effective use of meeting time, the company will be able to improve the service it delivers to its customers. Using the calculations above, the average employee will be able to spend an additional

$10 of his or her time per day meeting the market needs. (IR, IS: increase revenue, improve service)

Notice how concrete these objectives are. Business objectives should be as quantifiable as possible, so as to provide the criteria for judging the success of the intervention after it is implemented. They also provide the cost-benefit analysis that enables you to build a collaborative working relationship with the budget client.

Documenting the Learning Objectives

Creating learning objectives can be time consuming. Below is a simplified version of more academic approaches to creating objectives. Create good learning objectives by specifying the audience and behavior:

- Audience (A): Who will be learning? Whom is this objective for?
- Behavior (B): What will the learner be able to do differently, and how? How will the facilitator know that this learning has occurred? How will the business know?
- Condition (C): Under what conditions will the learning be required?

In the fictional case study offered earlier in the chapter, the reason underlying the project is a need to create behavioral change. The learning objectives are the criteria that define the work to be done, and at the end, determine whether the project has been implemented in a way that meets the clients' needs; they therefore should specify the desired behavior. An objective for the fictional case example might be, "After completing the workshop, the business staff member will be able to plan, from memory, the five preparation activities required for a successful meeting." Here, A is the business staff member, and B is the ability to plan from memory the five preparation activities required for a successful meeting.

Great learning events are driven by well thought-out learning objectives that meet two criteria:

1. The learning must be observable in the learning event (that is, the learner must be able to demonstrate that he or she can do each learning objective).

2. The learning must be measurable (the learner must be able to be tested on the thoroughness of the learning). Making the audience and behavior as explicit as possible enables measurement.

Behavior will reflect three types of learning:

- Skills: Will the learner be able to do something new?

- Knowledge: What level of expertise will the learner have?

- Attitude: Will the learner have a new belief?

Most learning in business requires all three types of learning, but developing new attitudes is an often overlooked but prevalent need that also is the most difficult learning to transfer.

Refer to the fictional case example—the executives would like the managers to be taught how to hold meetings that are effective and efficient. The list below contains the behavior changes the executives might like to see after training; the types of learning required are in parentheses:

- The managers will be able to use our meeting scheduling software to schedule a meeting. (knowledge, skill)

- The managers will create a properly sized meeting agenda. (knowledge, skill)

- The managers will estimate the appropriate time for a meeting. (knowledge, skill)

- The managers will choose to take the time to create the above meeting deliverables. (attitude)

- The managers will believe that effective and efficient meetings are possible. (attitude)

As you read through the list, notice that the most important outcomes—the ones that most closely map to the business' needs—are the ones that are attitudinal learning. In fact, if the managers don't believe in effective meeting management, they will never open up enough to learn the knowledge and skills specified in the first three outcomes.

When you ask your customers to describe how they want behaviors to change after a learning event, many will list skills and knowledge and leave out the attitude-related changes. Ask questions to ensure that the customers have considered all the attitude issues.

It is essential to good project management to create explicit learning objectives. Balance writing the perfect objective with the need to deliver learning in a timely manner. Don't spend so much time on objectives that you never deliver a learning event! At the other extreme, don't become immersed in course development and fun exercises, neglecting learning objectives altogether. Learning objectives are key to managing the scope of a learning event project and are an important factor in successful project management.

Documenting Scope

As you may already know, "scope creep" is the number one killer of projects. No matter what a project manager does, the business needs for the learning event will change over the duration of the project. The longer the project, the more likely the needs will change drastically. Scope cannot be frozen any more than business change can be eliminated. The best tactic for an effective project manager is to manage the scope so that change is understood by all.

At the start of the project, the project manager, the customer, and any other project team members must document the scope as they understand it. The more stakeholders who contribute to creating this document, the more unmistakable it will be to everyone when the scope changes as the project progresses. The best way to create this document is through a visual, high-level picture (more than two-thirds of all people are visual learners; that is, they prefer to learn something new through seeing). Many learning event developers make the mistake of creating scope documents out of written, boring text. Many customer approval sign-offs occur just to avoid the torture of reading the document.

Figure 2.1 is a sample scope diagram for the fictional case study described earlier. This example is basic, but your models should actually show the names of the groups or people with whom you will be working and the kind of information you will get from them. You can also add which learning objectives are geared toward which customers by indicating them on the arrows going out to the customers. Doing so will give you a complete diagram of the scope of the project.

As the project progresses and the business needs change, the learning objectives and the scope diagram will be updated. You'll read more about this process in chapter 5.

Figure 2.1. Sample scope diagram based on fictional case study described in the chapter.

The square boxes show the stakeholder interfaces to the project—the arrows to and from the boxes show where the information about the required learning comes from, how the learning event will be delivered, and who will receive the learning. The rounded box represents the scope of the project. The "inside" details of the project are unclear at the start, but the interfaces should be defined carefully.

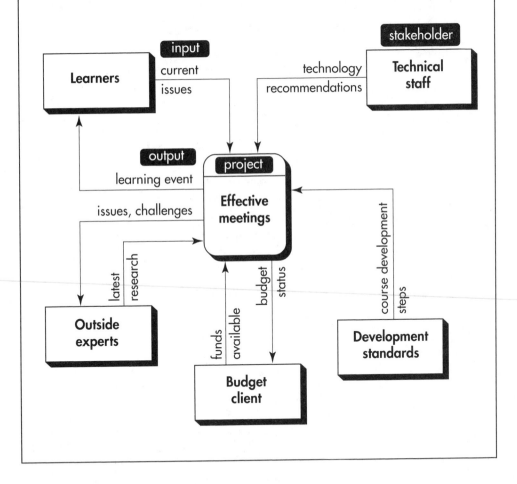

Documenting Risks

Risk is simply the likelihood that your project will fail in some way. It could fail to meet the learning needs of the customers, be late, or end up over budget. The higher the risk, the more likely that one of those problems will happen. Consequently, the higher the risk, the more time the project manager must spend on project management activities such as status meetings, troubleshooting the schedule or budget, evaluating quality, and other activities necessary to plan, organize, and control the learning event development project. In other words, the more risk, the more time that must be spent on project management.

Risk is inevitable, but analyzing and managing risk up front allows a project manager to do the following:

- Anticipate situations, glitches, and problems as well as build contingency plans

- Conduct project management activities in proportion to the amount of risk (for example, the greater the risk, the greater the number of status meetings)

- Manage the expectations of the stakeholders and the project team

- Challenge the mental models of the business customers.

Risk is reduced when more highly experienced people execute the project. Inexperienced developers, customers, and technical staff can severely slow a learning event project. Below is a "quick-and-dirty" risk assessment technique to calculate the risk of your project relative to other projects in which you and your team may have been involved. Once again, this technique works best if you do it with your entire project team and your customers, including the budget client.

Ask each participant to privately write down his or her answers to the following three questions:

1. How big is this project compared with others you have been part of? (A 1 indicates that it's the smallest, and a 10 indicates that it's the largest.)

2. How well do you understand the requirements for this project compared with other projects you have been part of? (A 1 indicates that the needs are completely clear, and a 10 indicates that the needs are undefined.)

3. How experienced are you with the technology you will use for this project? (A 1 indicates considerable experience with the technology, and a 10 indicates no knowledge of the technology.)

Now ask the participants to average their answers and then share them as a team. Like the other deliverables you have created so far, this is an important step toward managing the expectations of all your stakeholders.

Sample Risk Assessment

Think back to the fictional case example presented earlier in this chapter. Here is how such a risk assessment might work out for that case:

1. Size = 2	Since it is limited to one hour of learning, this is a fairly small learning event.
2. Requirements = 5	People have been studying effective meeting management for years, so although the project manager may not yet know exactly what the contents will be, it shouldn't be too hard to research this topic.
3. Technology = 1	This is going to be an instructor-led workshop, so the only technology needed will be basic.

Average = 2.4

To summarize, this is a fairly low-risk project that shouldn't require a lot of tight project management after the initial definition phase. If any of the assumptions change, however, the risk will change as well.

To show how the situation could get messy, suppose the decision is made that the training will no longer be instructor led but will be implemented on the company intranet as Web-based instruction. Technology now jumps to a 10, changing the average to 5.6. The project is now more likely to run into some surprises, especially where technology issues are concerned. The project manager must plan to pay careful attention to the technology component because it could seriously affect the success of this project.

To make things even more complicated, suppose the decision is made that the managers will build the meeting guidelines as a team rather than use research from outside sources. This approach will generate multiple meetings, conflict, and more politics and would change the requirements rating to 9, resulting in an average of 4. Again, the project manager would need to spend a great deal of energy on the requirements of the project to ensure success.

Scenario Planning

Another option for risk management is the use of scenario planning, which is a little more detailed. This section describes how to apply this powerful technique for learning organization skills.

First, gather the project team together and ask them to list glitches that occurred in other projects on which they worked, especially problems they wish they had foreseen at the beginning of the project. Then, ask them to brainstorm other surprises that might occur during the current project that relate to people, processes, organizational issues, or technology. Use this brainstormed list to create a table like the one in figure 2.2. Each scenario should be rated by the group for its possible effect on the project. Low-impact scenarios can be ignored. High- and, if time allows, medium-impact scenarios should generate a brief discussion of a contingency plan. The team has the option of creating either a preventive or a reactive response to the scenario; sometimes creating both makes sense. For example, suppose the project manager leaves. A preventive response would be to cross-train a backup project manager from the start; a reactive response would be to freeze the project while the new project manager is brought up to speed.

Risk-scenario planning is a wonderful technique that gives project managers the following benefits:

- It allows the entire project team to have common, realistic expectations.
- It drives more accurate (and less idealistic) estimating in the next phase.
- It removes "blinders" and helps the project manager anticipate and look for symptoms of glitches, thereby speeding reaction time to problems.

Risk management is an essential responsibility of a project manager. Having a consensus risk rating as a baseline provides two important success factors: 1) a clear understanding by all team members and stakeholders at the start and 2) a clear, shared strategy for managing the riskier aspects of the project as it progresses.

Documenting Constraints

All projects are constrained by time, money, and quality. The constraints should drive the manner in which the project is managed. A project to build a course for surgeons on the use of a complicated instrument for brain

Figure 2.2. Sample risk-scenario planning table.

Risk Factors	Likelihood	Impact	Action
Production platform changes during project	M	M	Add time for training on new technology
Project manager (PM) gets transferred	L	H	Plan meetings for backup to PM
People resources not available	M	H	Prioritize activities to cut if insufficient resources

H = High
M = Medium
L = Low

surgery should be managed entirely differently from a course for managers on how to fill out their time sheets. As part of the project charter, your team and stakeholders can use the technique described below to capture the prioritized constraints at the start. Once again, this visual document can be used throughout the project to identify whether any of the constraints have changed.

Figure 2.3 shows the consensus of the project team as to the constraints for the meeting management case example presented in this chapter. Quality is the first priority, because the material and presentation is vital to enabling attitude change throughout the company. Time is the second priority because clearly, a great deal of time is wasted. Cost is third because the longer the meetings go on in their current unproductive fashion, the more money the customer loses.

This visual aid will be useful for organizing and controlling your response to surprises in the manage phase (see chapter 5). For example, if

Figure 2.3. Sample table illustrating the consensus of a project team as to the constraints for a project.

Here, quality is the first priority, time is the second priority, and cost is the third priority. Visual aids such as this can be used throughout a project to help identify whether any constraints have changed.

Constraints

	Priority		
	First	**Second**	**Third**
Time		X	
Cost			X
Quality	X		

the constraints for the case example are true, then the project may well cost more or take a little more time than originally planned. Alternatively, quality can be maintained by cutting the scope of the project, which would not increase time or cost. When faced with a lack of time or money, a smaller piece can be delivered without compromising quality. For example, the meeting management materials might end up becoming a job aid rather than an instructor-led workshop.

To create this constraint matrix, ask each person to select his or her first, second, and third priority privately and then share the results as a team. The entire group must agree on the priorities before the project can continue. I have had situations in which the customers were in direct conflict with each other over what the priorities were. If this is the case, the conflicts must be resolved before proceeding, even if it requires escalating to higher levels of management to do it. No project can succeed when serving two different priorities.

Creating a Stakeholder Communication Plan

The success of a project often depends as much on the stakeholders and their perceptions as it does on the project manager and real work. A terrible mistake that many people make as they manage development projects for learning events is that they neglect to communicate proactively with the stakeholders. A stakeholder communication plan lays the groundwork for consensus and buy-in on an ongoing basis.

The scope diagram discussed earlier (see figure 2.1) is a good starting place for a communication plan. Each square represents people with whom communication is essential. With a little additional brainstorming, other people can be added to the list who are less directly affected by the project but who are nevertheless important to its success. Figure 2.4 is a sample communication plan for the meetings case study project used in this chapter. An up-front plan forces you to think about the specific information that each stakeholder needs and when. If in doubt, always err on the side of too much information.

People tend to prefer either visual (as you read earlier), kinesthetic (learning by doing), or auditory (learning by hearing) communication. Few people are equally proficient at all three. Consider the style of the person with whom you are communicating and gear your communication to that (for information on how to assess learning styles, you may want to look at my earlier book, *The Accelerated Learning Fieldbook*). For example, an auditory budget client may be happiest with a phone call detailing the challenges to the budget. A visual executive may want to see a pie chart of the same information.

Evaluate Alternatives

Note that in the fictional case example, a decision was made to use instructor-led delivery before the project began. Although this is not the optimum time to make such a decision, it is common. If possible, it is better to make the delivery decision later and to base it on the objectives, scope, risk, and constraints.

Figure 2.4. Sample stakeholder communication plan.

Columns two and three help gear the communication to the specific business and learning goals of each stakeholder. For example, the business manager and learners need to know in advance the plans for alpha and beta testing of the new learning event, but the executives and budget client probably do not. IRACIS = increase revenue/avoid cost/improve service.

Stakeholder	Business Objective	Goal	Communication	Frequency
Budget client	Avoid cost	Meet budget	Budget status	Monthly
			Return on investment	Monthly
Business manager	Improve service	Build capacity	Roll-out plan	After design
Learners	Improve service	Learning objectives	Learning objectives	After analysis
			Alpha, beta schedule	Mid-design
			Roll-out plan	After design
Executives	IRACIS	Build business	Status: learning objectives, schedule, and budget	Monthly
Developers	Improve service	Deliver quality, timely work	Need for services and timeline	After analysis, design (revised)
Technical staff	Improve service	Deliver quality, timely work	Need for services and timeline	After analysis, design (revised)
Outside experts	Increase revenue through visibility	Make business contacts	Need for research	At start of project
			Thanks	After analysis

Typical modes for delivering learning events include the following:

- Instructor-led learning
- Self-paced, paper-based learning
- Self-paced, computer or Web-based learning
- Self-paced, video-based learning
- Self-paced, audiotape based learning
- Combination learning: self-paced with sharing over the Web or in person
- Simulation or practicum (for example, learning games).

Consider how the cost and constraints of each alternative relate to the business and learning objectives as well as the information you gathered about the audience when building the learning objectives.

Summary

In this chapter, you have read about how to define a project. Asking the right questions of the right people can create an environment for success. Managing the scope, risks, and constraints of a project depend on a mutually agreed-upon baseline. If you skip this phase, your project will surely run over in time, quality, scope, or cost, if not all four. A little time at the beginning can save a tremendous amount of time and stress later. In the exercise below, you can practice the techniques you just read about on your own project.

Practical Exercises

Think about your own project for a moment and consider how you might put into practice the define phase described in this chapter. Exercises have been provided for you to create the following deliverables from this phase:

- The business objectives of the learning event project
- The learning objectives of the learning event
- The scope of the learning event project
- The risk and constraints of a learning event project
- A stakeholder communication plan.

Exercise 2.1: Creating the business objectives.

What is the business reason for your project?

Is the project a reaction to a government regulation or to competition?

Consider how this project will increase revenue, avoid cost, and improve service (remember the IRACIS mnemonic). The section in this chapter on business objectives can provide you with sample business objectives. List your project's business objectives here:

_____

_____

_____

_____

_____

_____

_____

_____

_____

_____

_____

_____

_____

_____

_____

_____

_____

Exercise 2.2: Creating the learning objectives.

As stated in the earlier section, learning objectives define the performance improvement on which the learning event will be measured.

What will it look like when the participants have completed the training?

How will they behave differently?

How will you observe whether this behavior has changed during the learning event?

Remember to specify

- A (the audience to which the learning is targeted),
- B (the behavior change), and
- C (the conditions under which the behavior will change, and to what extent).

Write your learning objectives below:

_____

_____

_____

_____

_____

_____

_____

_____

_____

_____

_____

_____

Exercise 2.3. Create a scope diagram.

Write the name of your project in the center box and write the names of the stakeholders in the other boxes. Show the inputs and outputs from stakeholders by drawing directional arrows between the boxes and the center box. Feel free to add more boxes if necessary. (Refer to the section on creating a scope diagram for more guidelines.)

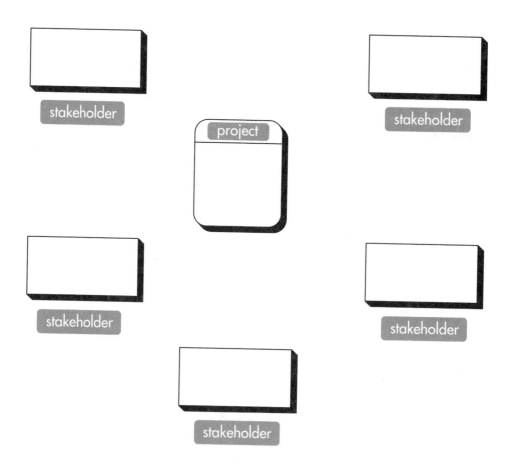

Exercise 2.4. Quick assessment.

Use this template to quickly assess the risk of your own project by rating its size, structure, and technology (see figure 2.2).

	Small									Huge
Size	1	2	3	4	5	6	7	8	9	10

	Defined									Unclear
Structure/requirements	1	2	3	4	5	6	7	8	9	10

	Known									Unknown
Technology	1	2	3	4	5	6	7	8	9	10

Average = ☐

Exercise 2.5. Risk-scenario planning.

Brainstorm some events that could dramatically raise the risk of your project and write them in the first column of the scenario table below. Rate the potential effects of each event on your project as high, medium, or low (H, M, or L). For the high-impact scenarios, briefly sketch out a plan of action and decide whether it is preventative, reactive, or both (see figure 2.2 as well as the section on risk for guidance).

Risk Factors	Likelihood	Impact	Action

Exercise 2.6. Prioritize your constraints.

Use this chart to create a visual representation of the priorities of the time, cost, and quality constraints your project faces.

Constraints

	Priority		
	First	Second	Third
Time			
Cost			
Quality			

Exercise 2.7. Draft a stakeholder communication plan.

List the stakeholders you identified in exercise 2.3 in the first column. Include any other people who will be interested in the progress of your project. For each stakeholder, consider what type of communication is needed and how frequently it must occur. Briefly note high-level ideas for specific communication for each stakeholder.

Stakeholder Communication Plan

Stakeholder	Business Objective	Goal	Communication	Frequency

Chapter 3

Planning the Project

Q: Why do course developers work on the wrong things at the wrong time?

A: They don't take the time to build a detailed enough plan of the work to be performed.

In this chapter you will learn how to carry out the following planning steps:

- Determine the tasks that need to be performed by the project manager and those that should be performed by a developer.
- Build a project plan for learning event development.
- Finalize the business objectives of the learning project.
- Create a work breakdown structure to uncover the activities needed to complete a project.
- Create critical path networks and Gantt charts as part of a project plan.
- Estimate the cost of training projects.
- Accurately estimate work effort for a project.

Building the Project Plan

When you really enjoy doing course development, you tend to look at new projects with idealistic optimism. It is essential, however, to take an honest look at what you are up against at the start. In chapter 2, you learned how to start a learning event project in a way that maximizes your chances for success—by building a document that defined the scope and boundaries of a project.

The project definition created in the last chapter is wonderful for managing and understanding the business setting, including the risks and the constraints of your project, but it doesn't help you understand what to do first, or what to do after that. This chapter shows you how to build a detailed plan to manage your project based on the project definition you previously created. The plan that you build in this chapter will help you prioritize not only your efforts as project manager but also the efforts of the developers. In this document, often called the *project plan,* you work at the following tasks:

- Finalizing objectives
- Creating the work breakdown structure
- Creating the schedule
- Using the critical path method
- Estimating resources
- Assigning resources
- Assigning project-related work
- Evaluating environmental factors
- Creating Gantt charts
- Using project management software
- Creating the budget.

Remember that this thinking is, at best, educated guessing and, at worst, shooting in the dark. A project never flows exactly as planned. Most of your projects will require a major shift in strategy at some point. The main concept here is strategy—the project plan is your strategy, which is based on the project as you understand it at the outset. When your comprehension changes, your strategy may change as well. You will have a *new* project plan, but you will still *have* a project plan. I call this approach *flexible structure.* The key to successful project management of any kind is managing a flexible structure for your project.

Finalizing the Business and Learning Objectives

As you begin to do more research into the actual learning required for this project, you will discover more about the details of both the business and the learning objectives. It is not surprising to learn of new or changed business and learning objectives after the project has been approved. Often, the complicated or troublesome issues are not revealed to the developer or project manager until the project is well under way. People don't like to start with bad news. Expect surprises.

From the beginning it is vital to manage the scope of the project tightly. Keep your scope diagram handy throughout the project to ensure that everyone knows when you are adding new scope through new business or learning objectives. The development of the project plan is important because it is the first point at which you will be tested with new requirements. If the new objectives have added to your scope, negotiate the acquisition of appropriate additional resources, such as time and money.

Some Practical Help

Using the fictional case example presented in chapter 2 (developing a one-hour meeting management course), consider what might happen if the organization hired to write the meeting guidelines only focused on behavior during a meeting and not pre- and postmeeting activities. What would happen if your project was now responsible for developing pre- and post-meeting guidelines? Consider the answers to the following questions:

Q: Does this change affect the scope of the project? (Hint: check the diagram in figure 2.2.)

A: Yes—there are more sources from which to gather information about pre- and postmeeting activities

Q: If yes, how does it affect the scope? Will the project require more or less work?

A: The project will require more work—specifically, in the course development around the pre- and postmeeting activities.

Q: Will it be necessary to create new business objectives? New learning objectives?

The answer to the last question is yes. This addition significantly changes the scope of the development work because a new business objective has been added to the trainer's portion of the project: To avoid the labor cost of lost productivity in meetings, the business will now need to develop documented and thorough pre- and postmeeting activities. Surprisingly enough, the learning objectives are not affected because pre- and postmeeting activities were already included in the original scope. Business change (for example, a change in who will provide the requirements) generally has a larger effect on the scope than other changes.

After you determine what development activities will be required to complete the project, you must determine how long each activity will take and how many resources you will need. You also must consider obtaining an agreement with the customer on the project scope. Before going forward with any planning on the project, make sure all parties agree to the list of business and learning objectives. Although the list may change, a baseline is essential in order to negotiate for additional resources when change does occur.

Creating the Work Breakdown Structure

A work breakdown structure (WBS) is a hierarchical chart that helps you brainstorm activities that need to be completed for a project. Figure 3.1 shows a generic WBS for a learning event—in this case, course development. (You'll learn about a more detailed template for learning event development in chapter 4.) Your chart will usually be more detailed than this one and may include additional activities that are required for your specific business need. You create a WBS from your organization's course development standard and your experiences. Your experiences are as valuable as any model would be.

When building a WBS, brainstorm the components of each activity to a level detailed enough for you to estimate how long it will take to complete each activity. As shown in figure 3.1, "develop a learning event" breaks down into four activities, each of which is too general to estimate accurately and must be broken down further. "Create skills practice" consists of two steps: "honor multiple intelligences" and "honor the environment." These detailed activities can be scheduled and estimated.

You may find that you are not comfortable thinking in a top-down fashion such as this. Some people prefer brainstorming at a detailed level, with piles of Post-its, and then grouping them from the bottom up into a WBS. Others prefer to begin in the middle and work both up and down. Whichever method fits your personal style is the right one for you to use. If you are part

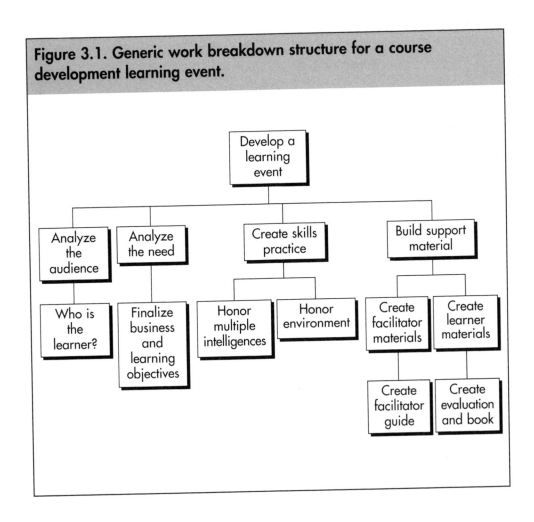

Figure 3.1. Generic work breakdown structure for a course development learning event.

of a team, remember to honor the needs of other team members to process in different ways.

Sharing these charts with other people may help you discover gaps in your thought process. Even if you have to do the project alone, consider borrowing the brains of your friends to help you with this strategic planning activity. The following checklist can help you build a successful WBS:

- Have you considered project management activities such as status meetings, reviews, and the construction of stakeholder communication plans?

- Have you considered all the activities that will have to be done by people outside your direct influence, such as printing, design, programming, or video work?

- Have you considered all the research that you will need to do?

- Who will present the finished learning event? Will there need to be training notes or other instruction for people who will present the event?

- Have you considered how you will test the learning before it is implemented?

The WBS is not a diagram that you maintain for long. Its purpose is to help you brainstorm the activities that will go into the schedule in the next step. The schedule is the guide and is changed and adjusted. The WBS is just a stepping stone toward the schedule. If you find it easier to brainstorm in other ways, this step can be replaced with other techniques. For wonderful brainstorming alternatives, I recommend the book *Thinkertoys*, by Michael Michalko (Berkeley, CA: Ten Speed Press, 1991).

Creating the Schedule

The schedule comprises three parts:

- the activities that need to be completed,

- the sequence of the activities, and

- the time required for each activity and the people who will do the work.

The activities that need to be completed are established either through a WBS or through another brainstorming technique that you prefer. The sequence of the activities is best shown with a critical path diagram, which illustrates the activities that are the most critical and the ones that depend on other activities.

Figure 3.2 shows the beginning of a critical path diagram based on the generic WBS in figure 3.1. Notice that this diagram shows that some activities must be completed before others can begin. By definition, if one activity follows another and is connected with a dependency, the first activity must be completely finished before the next can begin (although in practice, dependent activities often can be started before their predecessors are completely finished). This diagram shows that some activities can be done in tandem, some can start at any time, and others must wait for predecessor activities. This type of predecessor dependency is often called *task dependency* or *activity dependency*. In addition, as people are assigned to

Figure 3.2. Sample critical path diagram.

Each box contains an activity based on a work breakdown structure (see figure 3.1). Dependencies—activities that cannot begin until a previous activity is completed—are shown with arrows. In this case, the path along the bottom of the diagram is the critical path, because it requires the most time to complete. The shortest path, the one at the top of the diagram, contains the project's slack time, which is the difference between the longest path and the shortest path. Milestones are indicated by "0d."

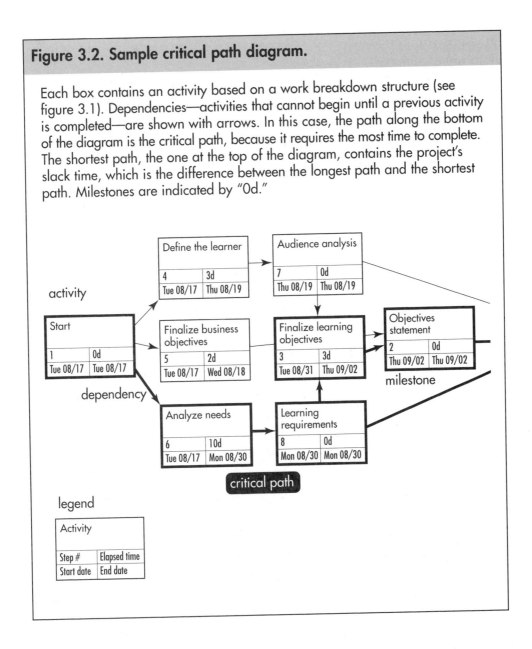

activities, new dependencies may emerge. One person cannot work on two different activities at the same time, so a choice must be made to place one ahead of the other. This situation is called *people dependency*. Later in this chapter you will read more about allocating people resources.

Milestones are not real activities and do not take any time (note the 0 days needed for "audience analysis"). The milestones provide the project manager with a place to stop and check progress. In some situations, milestones may be approval points at which contracted work is paid for or interim deliverables are completed.

The next step is to estimate how long each activity will take. The estimate will depend on the complexity of the activity, the expertise of the person or people working on it, the number of people and organizations involved, and the culture of the company where the work is to be performed. The next section describes a process for realistic estimating, which takes all of these elements into account.

Estimating

To estimate requires a little math and a lot of experience. Expertise allows you to more accurately estimate based on your previous project work. Common sense and history are the best ingredients for accurate estimates.

There are two different types of estimates: *duration* and *elapsed time.* Duration is how long an activity would take if a person of average experience worked on it nonstop, without any interruptions. For example, below are guidelines for the duration of common types of course development projects:

Instructor-led training	15 hours of development for 1 hour of instruction
Computer-based training	200 hours of development for 1 hour of instruction

Obviously, no developer can work on something for 200 hours without stopping. This is where the second kind of estimating, elapsed time, comes into play. Elapsed time is the amount of calendar or clock time that will pass before the activity is completed. For example, the 200 hours of development for a computer-based training in the example above might actually take 10 weeks of elapsed time. Elapsed time is calculated using three add-ons to duration: expertise, project-related work, and environmental factors.

Expertise. Expertise can significantly lengthen or shorten the duration of an activity. For example, a person who has never done computer-based training development will take much longer to complete one hour of instruction than a person who has been developing this kind of training for many years. Two different kinds of expertise must be taken into account: expertise in the activity and expertise in the content. The example just cited is expertise in the activity (that is, computer-based training development expertise). Similarly, if you have a choice between two developers, one who has significant knowledge of the content of the learning material and one who does not, you will choose the developer with knowledge. He or she will take less elapsed time to complete the project and will not have to perform as much research or needs analysis because of his or her expertise. Think back to the fictional case example presented in chapter 2. If the scope changes to include a computer-based learning event, knowledge of good meeting guidelines would be an example of content expertise.

One of the most influential factors in elapsed time is the level of expertise of the people performing a project activity. Based on my experience, I apply a factor of 0.5 to 4.0 percent. Before you can judge the elapsed time of an activity, you must find out (or decide) who will be working on it. To adjust for expertise in the activity, the project manager multiplies the estimated duration by 0.5 to 1.5, with 0.5 representing people with a great deal of expertise and 1.5 representing people with no expertise. After inflating the estimated duration with the activity expertise factor, the project manager factors in content expertise by multiplying the new estimate by 0.75 to 4.0 (high content expertise to low content expertise).

Let's assume our developer has average experience in computer-based development but no expertise in the content. The calculation would be as follows:

Duration = 200 hours

Activity expertise = 1.0

Subtotal (200×1) = 200 hours

Content expertise = 4.0

Adjusted duration (4.0×200) = 800 hours

Project-Related Work. The second add-on is project-related work. This is the amount of time you add to the duration for the communication necessary to ensure a successful project. This figure is most influenced by the number of people involved in the project. Obviously, an activity that will be performed by one developer and one content expert will take less time than the same activity done by three developers with three content experts from three different departments. As the number of players and organizations ratchets up, communication takes exponentially more time. On the basis of my experience, a factor of .10 (fewer players) to .20 (more players) should be added to the duration after the expertise add-on (discussed in the previous section).

Continuing our example and assuming that we have one developer and one content expert:

Adjusted duration after expertise add-on: 500 hours

Adjustment for project-related communication factor = 0.15:
 (500 × 0.15 = 75 hours)

New adjusted duration (500 + 75) = 575 hours

Environmental Factors. The last add-on is for environmental factors, which are actually nonproject activities. This add-on (a factor of 0.25 to 0.35) is needed because the project exists in a business that requires its employees to do other tasks besides project work, such as check and respond to their voice or email. It also builds in a cushion for illness, vacations, and events like company meetings. The best way for a project manager to estimate how much should be added for this factor is to track what percentage of the workday, on average, is devoted to nonproject work. For example, if you work an eight-hour day and can usually spend six hours on project work, you have 25 percent overhead for environmental work. This add-on will be the same for each activity, so many project managers add an activity for 25 percent of the adjusted duration before each milestone instead of inflating each activity. It is important to remember that this factor is not fluff and is not a safety net for project problems. It is the actual time that is going to be used for non-project-related activities. Returning to our example, the final adjustment is as follows:

Adjusted duration so far: 575 hours

Environmental adjustment factor = 0.25:
 (575 × 0.25 = 143.75)

Elapsed time (575 + 143.75) = 718.75 hours

Essentially, this estimating method converts duration to elapsed time. Duration does not tell how long it will actually take to finish a task. This is a common mistake and can cause confusion if these adjustments aren't included. If you think your project is going to take the total of all the activity *duration*—say, 40 hours—you will be upset when you find that projects actually take the *elapsed* time of all activities, which might be as much as 200 percent more. This is how many projects get into trouble. No one can work on a project without spending time on other tasks at the same time, so careful estimating techniques truthfully acknowledging the real world are an essential factor for successful projects.

At this point, it is time to add the people dependencies and the elapsed time estimates to the critical path diagram. When there is more than one parallel path, one path usually has a longer total elapsed time than the other. The longest path is called the *critical path*. The shortest path has *slack time*, which is the difference between the longest path and the shortest path. In other words, the shortest path has a little extra time, but this extra time is for the whole path, not each activity, which is a common misconception. Many project management software packages mislead the user into thinking that each activity on the path has the same slack time, when it actually is the entire path that has that much slack time. The project manager can check progress of the project against the critical path diagram shown in figure 3.2 because it clearly illustrates the dependencies of the activities. This type of diagram is excellent for monitoring the work on the critical path, which when late, is most detrimental to the success of the entire project.

Program evaluation and review technique (PERT) charts are special cases of critical path diagrams that are laid out with a timeline across the bottom. This adds a management dimension that is missing from a critical path diagram. Many people prefer to use a separate diagram called a Gantt chart for this view.

Gantt Charts

A project manager needs to be able to manage a timeline and needs to know what activities should be happening at any given point in time. This calendar view is often represented with a chart called a bar chart or Gantt chart. Gantt charts can represent different views of the project activity against a calendar. Figure 3.3 shows an example of a Gantt chart.

Gantt charts can be used to show when each activity will start and should end and who is assigned to work on each activity. In simpler projects, this can be combined into one chart like that shown in figure 3.4. In more complex projects, Gantt charts may be organized by milestones. This type of chart also can be made for each person working on the project, with just his or her activities shown. When the charts are separated, however, it can be difficult for a project member to see the critical activities and their dependencies. As the project struggles and the project manager needs to reassign people, the original critical path diagram can be used to stay focused on

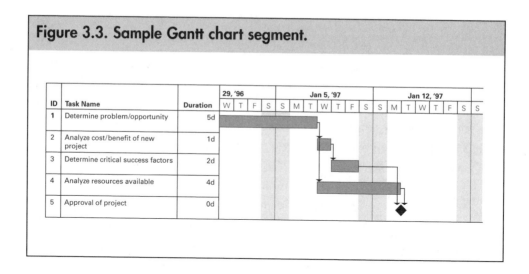

Figure 3.3. Sample Gantt chart segment.

dependencies, and the Gantt chart can be used to monitor elapsed time and how much work each person has been assigned (people load).

Project Management Software

If your project is fairly complex, you may find it helpful to use a project management software package to create a plan that is visually pleasing and easy to change. Some software products, such as Microsoft Project, keep all your information in one place but allow you to view it in different ways.[1] You

Figure 3.4. Sample Gantt chart segment for a simple project.

---

[1] A number of project management software packages are available; see the resource list at the back of the book.

can look at your project as a critical path diagram, as a Gantt chart, from the perspective of individual assignments, and by dates, in almost any combination. Here are some tips to help you decide whether and how to use software:

- Using project management software can be time consuming. Sometimes you can find that you have wasted a lot of time trying to do something that the software cannot easily do, if at all. Limit your time on the computer so you don't end up doing project management software work instead of project work.

- Sometimes, if your project is small risk, a simple drawing is all you need to manage the project. A good drawing package, without all the calculations and logic of project management software, may be enough to make it pretty but will not add so much complexity that it takes your attention away from the project.

- Consider asking someone else to actually enter your hand-drawn project plans into the computer. That way, you can stay focused on project management and the other person can help you with administration.

- A good guideline for project management software is to let the software calculate dates from your activity estimates as much as possible. Doing so gives the software more flexibility to adjust the dates when actual activity time is greater or less than planned. You will learn more about actual activity duration and its effect in chapter 5.

Creating the Budget

The more complex the project, the more important it is to manage the budget carefully. The budget worksheet in figure 3.5 is an example of a worksheet used to document the budget at the start of the project and then manage the budget as actual project work is completed. Using worksheet software can make this easier to manage.

If you are the only person on the project, you may not find it necessary to be this rigorous in your management of the budget. Remember the discussion of constraints in the define phase (see chapter 2); in many cases, learning event developers are assigned a fixed budget and have no ability to get more funding, even if they need it. In this case, the project manager is better served by monitoring scope and critical path than by monitoring the budget. (Chapter 5 provides more information on this topic.)

Figure 3.5. Sample worksheet for documenting the budget at the start of a project and managing the budget as actual project work is completed.

Expense Item	Projected Cost (complete during plan phase)	Actual Cost (complete during manage phase)
Labor • People • Contractors • Vendors		
Environment • Work space • Supplies • Computer equipment • Software • Services		
Process • Books • Methodology • Training		
Organization • Meeting expenses • Conference calls • Travel • Room rental • Refreshments		
Expample: • Contractors	$ 50,000	$ 75,000

History Says . . .

Some lessons I have learned about creating a project plan for course development projects are as follows:

- It always takes longer than you think it will. This is generally a result of events not immediately under your control, including business politics, other people, and surprises such as weather, illness, and even promotions. These glitches will not take long to emerge, and may hit the day you start. Don't get discouraged—plan for them. The risk assessment process (see chapter 2) should help you deal realistically with changes and surprises. They *will* happen.

- It is tempting, no matter how experienced you are, to skip the planning step. In fact, the more experienced you are, the more tempted you will be to skip it. Don't. Even if you never look at the plan again, creating the plan will dramatically improve your project success because it will influence the approach you take.

- If you do not believe the plan is possible, you're right. Be honest with yourself and to anyone who is trying to coerce you into a schedule that you do not think is possible.

- Everyone's expectations—yours, the customers, and the other team members—are strongly influenced by a common visual picture and language. The project plan creates a central place of understanding and should be a living, breathing, evolving document as the project progresses.

Summary

In this chapter, you read about how to plan a learning event project. To manage a project as it progresses requires a clear, detailed plan specifying the activities to be completed, the order in which they will be done, the people who will work on them, and the time each will take. Milestones, status checks, and budget worksheets are especially important for complex projects.

Practical Exercises

Now practice the plan phase activities you have just learned. Again, you can take maximum advantage of this book by using your own project as a reference point. In the following exercises, use the forms provided to plan your own project.

Exercise 3.1: Finalizing objectives.

Before you begin, take a look at the business and learning objectives you created for your own project in the practice exercises in chapter 2. Consider the following questions:

Q: Are these objectives still accurate? Are the measurements meaningful and possible?

A: If yes, great! You are in good shape. Remember, the objectives are your contract with your customer.

If no, get sign-off from your customer on the new objectives before proceeding.

Q: Do you need additional objectives now that you know more about the project?

A: If yes, great!

If no, consider revisiting the ABCs of good objectives in chapter 2.

Create a complete list of the revised objectives in the space below:

_____

_____

_____

_____

_____

_____

_____

_____

Exercise 3.2. Create a work breakdown structure (WBS).

Using the template shown, create a WBS for your own project. The levels have been provided for you as a guide only; add more boxes or leave boxes blank if needed, and work down as many levels as it takes to get to estimatable activities.

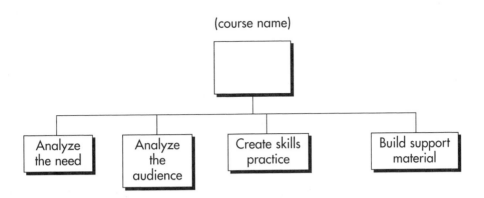

Exercise 3.3. Build a critical path diagram.

Use the blank template below to build a critical path diagram for your own project. Feel free to change the template as it makes sense for your project. Milestones can be identified by an elapsed time of zero.

Be mindful of any activity dependencies—are there any activities that can't start until others are completed?

Does it make sense to add some milestones along the way?

Starting Critical Path Diagram

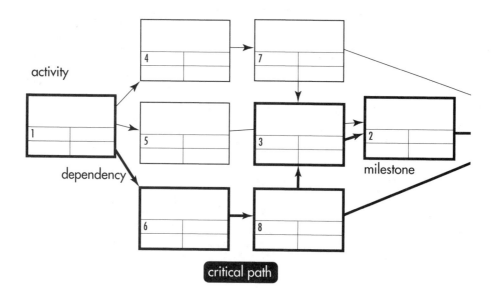

legend

Activity	
Step #	Elapsed time
Start date	End date

Exercise 3.4. Adjust project work estimates and revise the critical path diagram.

For each activity in the boxes in the critical path diagram:

1. Estimate the duration.
2. Assign one or more people to the activity, as needed.
3. Adjust the duration for the expertise of the people assigned.
4. Adjust the duration for the project-related factor.

Use this worksheet to perform your adjustments for each activity you listed in a box in exercise 3.3. When you have your final adjustments, change the critical path diagram according to the instructions in the exercise. Add the environmental factor either as a factor on each activity duration, as a new activity before each milestone, or as a new activity at the start of the project. Mark the critical path so you know which activities must be monitored the most carefully.

Step 1: Base work effort = ____ hours/days

Step 2: Skill/experience/knowledge level

Multiply by .75 to 4.0 for skill/experience level (high to low)

Skill/experience level = ____ × ____ base work effort = ____ new adjusted work effort

Multiply by .50 to 1.5 for job knowledge (high to low)

Job knowledge = ____ × ____ adjusted work effort = ____ new adjusted work effort

Step 3: Project-related factor = 10 to 20 percent

Project-related factor = (____ %) × ____ adjusted work effort + ____ adjusted work effort = ____ new adjusted work effort

Step 4: Environmental factor = 25 to 35 percent

Environmental factor = (____ %) × ____ adjusted work effort + ____ adjusted work effort = ____ new adjusted work effort

Revised Work Estimate = ____ hours/days

Exercise 3.5. Create a calendar timeline.

Based on your critical path diagram, use the blank Gantt chart to create a calendar timeline for your own project, beginning with the day you expect to start.

List the people who will be working on the project down the left side of the chart, with the calendar running from left to right. Block out any unavailable days for any of the resources (for example, weekends, holidays, and travel). Add the activities each person will be working on, honoring the dependencies of the critical path diagram. Then darken the activities of the critical path to remind yourself of what the most important activities are. You will almost certainly need to use a separate sheet to create your chart; if your project is complex, consider transferring it to software after you construct a prototype by hand.

Blank Gantt Chart

	(start date)			
Person 1				
Person 2				
Person 3				

Exercise 3.6: Creating a budget.

Use the blank budget worksheet to brainstorm the budget items of your own project and estimate the cost of this project. Consider both tangible costs, such as supplies and equipment, as well as intangible costs, such as people time.

Expense Item	Projected Cost	Actual Cost
Labor • People • Contractors • Vendors Environment • Work space • Supplies • Computer equipment • Software • Services Process • Books • Methodology • Training Organization • Meeting expenses • Conference calls • Travel • Room rental • Refreshments		

Chapter 4

A Course Development Template

Q: How can I remember what to do when?

A: Follow a flexible, repeatable process for development.

In this chapter, you will learn how to do the following:

- Build a project plan for a new learning event, course acquisition, or contracted training project.
- Choose the appropriate activities for each project.

In previous chapters, you read about the two initial phases of managing a development process: define and plan. Each systemically depends on the other. For example, you cannot build a plan without clearly understanding the questions answered in the define phase.

As you read about how to plan a project, you may have been a little confused about where the activities came from for creating and implementing a learning event. You may have a course development method that you already use, such as one that is required by your company's standards. This, then, is where you find the activities you use to build your plan. Development methodologies are created to consider all possibilities, however. You must be sure that the activities that don't make sense for your project are eliminated. Put another way, only plan activities that you are completely sure contribute to the project. Many novice developers try to follow standard methods blindly, spending valuable time on activities not pertinent to their projects.

Many of you may not have a standard development method available to you, or you may not like the one that you have. This chapter describes a method for creating learning events that is based on adult learning theories and accelerated learning. This approach emphasizes experiential learning, rather than lectures. For more on accelerated learning, check the resource list for other books on the topic, including mine. In this chapter, you will learn about the following tasks:

- The Learner First Approach
- Estimating resources
- Designing a repeatable but flexible process.

The Learner First Approach

The process that this chapter will explore is called The Learner First Approach (described in *The Accelerated Learning Fieldbook* [San Francisco: Jossey-Bass Pfeiffer, 1999]), a model of which is illustrated in figure 4.1.

Identify the Audience.

The first step of The Learner First Approach is to clearly define the audience that will be affected by the learning. You should consider four different audiences when you are creating a learning event:

- The learner: the person who needs to learn
- The budget client: the person who writes the check for the event
- The scheduler: the person who manages the logistics of the event
- The supervisor/manager: the person to whom the learner reports.

One person may play multiple roles, or multiple people may share one of these roles.

Although much of your development work will focus on the learning gap of the learner, both the budget client and the scheduler have needs that are as important as the learning needs of the student; for political reasons, you must meet those needs.

The learners can be defined by answering questions like the following:

- What are the age ranges of the people you expect in this workshop?
- Will the learners be male or female—or a combined group?

Figure 4.1. Model of The Learner First Approach.

Because memory is strengthened by review, the mnemonic "Accelerated Learning Offers Everyone Something Magically Effective" is included to help you remember the seven steps.

Accelerated	**A** Identify the udience	Who needs to learn?
Learning	**L** Identify earning need	What behavior will change?
Offers	**O** Create learning bjective	How will you measure the learning?
Everyone	**E** Create xercise	How can the learners learn through experiences?
Something	**S** equence learning objective	How can the flow enhance learning?
Magically	**M** Create support aterial	What other materials are needed?
Effective	**E** valuate the learning	How can learning improve?

ALOESME

- What is their educational background? Do they have high school degrees? College? What types of learning events have they been part of before, including workshops, computer-based training, video conferencing, Internet, and so forth?

- From what region or country are your learners? What are some norms that might affect their learning?

- From what ethnic background are your learners? What are some of the cultural norms that might affect their learning?

- From what industry will these people come? What industry norms might affect their learning?

- What is the corporate culture where the learners work? Does it encourage learning? What is their current workload? How focused can they be in class? Will they be able to do pre- or postclass work?

The needs of the budget client—that is, the person or department of the organization requesting the training—are completely focused on getting value out of the dollars invested. The budget client will be concerned about some of the following matters:

- What is the cost of the workshop? For example, some training suppliers charge per day of instruction, whereas others charge per learning event.

- Is there a limit to the number of learners you can have in the workshop? Is there an additional charge per learner after a certain enrollment has been reached?

- Are materials and books included in the cost figure, or will there be an additional charge?

- Is the travel expense for the learning facilitator included in the cost figure, or will there be an additional charge? Is there a ceiling on the travel expenses? What is covered?

- If the budget client commits to a certain volume of business, is there a discount?

- Is there a money-back guarantee?

- What is the policy for purchase orders and the timeframe for payment?

Begin your work with budget clients by asking them whom you should talk to about content questions. Content is not the role of the budget client and will require a subject matter expert.

The scheduler role is usually played by the training manager or an assistant. This contact can answer the following questions:

- Who is the subject matter expert?
- Who requested the training? Who can describe the learning gap?
- Where will the classes be held? Can you specifically request certain room setups?
- Where should the books and supplies be shipped?
- Can you arrange to get into the room an hour early for setup?
- Can you get a map to the training location? Where should you park?
- If relevant, what types of travel guidelines should the trainers follow (for example, corporate discount, hotel, rental car, airport transportation)?
- What will be the hours of the learning event? What time is lunch? Will food be provided for breaks?

Finally, the supervisor ultimately will be the judge of whether you have been successful with this effort. It is essential to establish this person's view of success early on. Ask the supervisor what the business will look like after the problem has gone away. Who and what will have to change for this to occur? What will the changes look like?

To summarize, identifying the audience typically involves the following four activities:

1. Identifying the people who play the roles of learner, budget client, scheduler, and supervisor.

2. Interviewing people in each role.

3. Synthesizing the results of all interviews.

4. Creating a statement that clearly describes the demographics of the target learner.

By defining the audience, you have begun to clarify the learning need. You now know which people can answer your questions and are prepared to gather more detailed information.

Identify the Learning Need

In this step, the course developer must determine the business problem that the company is trying to solve (see figure 4.1). Business reasons must drive learning objectives. Not only does this approach make the learning event easier to sell, it also ensures that the money being invested in the learning event is a good return for the company. Clarity about the business problem also guarantees that you can give the learners information that is "need-to-know," not "nice-to-know." You already may have completed business and learning objectives as part of the project charter in the define phase.

By clearly documenting the business reasons for the learning event, the course developer will have the criteria required to assess the benefit dollars from holding the training. In other words, the business reasons provide the framework to calculate return-on-investment. Business criteria also help the course developer clearly explain what other changes must take place in the business in order for the training to be effective. This performance consulting approach leverages the training to contribute measurable results to the bottom line.

The first two steps of The Learner First Approach—identify the audience and identify the learning needs—are what people mean when they say they are performing a needs analysis. In the next chapter, you will read about processes for needs analysis, whether broad (determine the needs or gaps present in the entire company) or specific (determine the needs for a particular workshop). Here is a list of typical activities associated with identifying learning needs:

- Document the business objectives and their measurements.
- List the people you will interview for detailed needs.
- Interview each person.
- Synthesize needs into one document.
- Ensure that each need maps to a business objective clearly.
- Ensure that each need belongs to one of the target audience members.

You now have all the information you need to begin the next step. The next section describes the most important part of course development: writing appropriate, concrete, and measurable learning objectives.

Create Learning Objectives

Once the business reason is clear and the needs are understood, the learning objectives (see chapter 2) can be created by clearly stating the audience and the behavior you will be able to observe during the learning event. The objectives provide guidance during the event for the course developer, facilitator, and learner. They are the core that drives the entire learning experience.

Create Exercises

Even when running an effective meeting instead of climbing a mountain, people learn best when they try it themselves. Regardless of whether your learning event will be delivered by a facilitator or a computer, learning by doing is the most effective way to learn. Many traditional course development methodologies encourage course developers to create lecture notes as soon as the learning objectives are finished, then create the exercises last. As in all projects, the items that are left for last are done least well. In The Learner First Approach, the exercises come before all the other support material, including lecture notes, to ensure that they are well planned and implemented. If the developer runs out of time, the lecture material is short-changed, instead of the practice. Activities associated with this step typically include the following:

- Create review sessions.
- Create debriefing questions.
- Create games or simulations.
- Validate the exercises against learning theories.
- Validate the exercises against the audience analysis and learning objectives.

The best learning occurs when learners discover knowledge themselves through an experience and then have time to reflect about what took place. The next step sequences those experiences.

Sequence the Learning Objectives

The next step of The Learner First Approach is to determine the order in which you will cover the learning objectives and the learning activities. A sense or intuition about sequencing comes from experience in the medium. That said, the guidelines discussed in this section will help you learn from others' experience if you have not had much up to this point.

Although it seems rational to start with the basics (such as terminology and introductory material) and move up to complex learning, it is usually more effective to begin with a comprehensive example and then present the pieces, referring back to the example. Learners respond to seeing the "big picture" first because it makes it easier for them to connect the terminology and concepts into a cohesive whole.

In addition, exercises should be sequenced based on how they honor the multiple intelligences. Howard Gardner[1] initially identified seven intelligences (now 10) that we all use to process information and think:

- Interpersonal: An aptitude for understanding other people and processing through interaction with them.

- Logical/mathematical: An aptitude for analytical thinking, calculations, and problem solving.

- Spatial/visual: An aptitude for designing, envisioning, and creating visual things.

- Musical: An aptitude for performing, listening to, and singing music.

- Linguistic/verbal: An aptitude for reading, writing, or speaking.

- Intrapersonal: An aptitude for personal reflection.

- Bodily/kinesthetic: An aptitude for movement.

The three newer intelligences proposed by Gardner in his 1996 white paper (see resource list) are

- emotional (an aptitude for identifying and reacting to your emotions),

- naturalist (an aptitude for being in touch with nature), and

- existential (an aptitude for understanding the purpose of your life).

Whenever possible, all intelligences should be stimulated in every experience in the learning event. Obviously, this is not always possible. When it is necessary to leave an intelligence out of an exercise, follow that exercise with another that contains the omitted intelligence. For example, follow heavily intensive team activities with intrapersonal reflection. Typical activities associated with the sequencing step are as follows:

---

[1] See the resource list for books by Gardner on the subject.

- sequence the learning objectives,
- sequence the exercise flow, and
- validate the exercises against Gardner's multiple intelligences.

Create Support Materials

The next-to-last step of The Learner First Approach is to determine the materials you will need to supplement the exercise so that the learning objectives are achieved. Today, you have myriad choices of support materials. Here is a list of typical activities associated with creating support materials:

- Create user guides, reference materials, learner guides, and prerequisite work.
- Design and create the presentation media (for example, overheads and PowerPoint slides).
- Create the facilitator notes.
- Detail the supplies you will need for each class.
- Design and distribute marketing information.
- Document the learning environment requirements (that is, the equipment, seating, refreshments, and other environmental requirements for each class).

Evaluate the Learning

The final step of The Learner First Approach is to continually monitor and make changes based on the successes or weaknesses of the learning event over its lifetime, regardless of how long the life is. The monitoring criteria are established by the learning objectives. Once you complete the learning event, it is tempting to think that you are finished, but the work is just beginning. A tremendous amount of attention has to be paid to keeping overheads, students' materials, and supplies consistent as you make changes. Think of your learning events as never finished and continually evolving. For example, consider the ripple effect of a change to one page of a presentation. It could also affect

- the overheads or slides;
- the facilitator notes;

- the prework;
- the exercises, games, and simulations;
- the marketing material;
- the supply list; and
- the room setup.

At this point in developing the learning event, establish a plan for ongoing evaluation of the workshop and how the maintenance of all the pieces will be handled. The initial rollout of the learning event is the first part of this plan. The best sequence of events for a rollout is as follows:

- Alpha class (first pilot): Facilitate the class with a group of experts, then update the workshop.
- Beta class (second pilot): Facilitate the class with a hand-picked group representing the target audience, then update the workshop.
- Production: Roll out the class for the main audience.

This procedure sounds wonderful, but in business you almost never get the time to do this type of rollout. You may be in a work environment demanding that your learning events hit the ground running; the two pilot classes therefore may not be feasible. To implement a learning event more quickly, substitute less time-intensive refinement by doing the following:

- Walk through the material, flow, and exercises with your learning peers.
- Try out as many of the exercises as possible with others.
- Walk through the material, flow, and exercises with a group of subject matter experts.
- Be prepared to change material after the first couple of workshops.
- Be prepared to change on the fly during the workshop (improvise).

Here is a list of typical activities associated with the evaluation step:

- Establish ongoing evaluation procedures.
- Plan the alpha class.
- Plan the beta class.

- Plan the production rollout.
- Walk through the material with peers.
- Make appropriate changes.
- Synchronize all support materials after changes.
- Establish maintenance procedures.

Estimating

As you have just read, only identifying the activities required to develop your learning event is not enough to build a project plan. It is also necessary to estimate the amount of time it will take to complete these activities. Chapter 3 provides detailed guidelines on how to estimate the time needed for a project (that is, how to convert duration to elapsed time). It is also essential to allocate time for estimating. When creating the project plan, incorporate periodic activities to do the following:

- Evaluate and monitor the actual durations of the activities currently under way
- Adjust future activity duration based on new knowledge.

In a sense, you must keep part of your mind focused on today's activities as well as anticipate changes on the basis of your experience.

A Repeatable but Flexible Process

Development methods have a light and dark side. The light side is that they provide a repeatable checklist that enables you to increase the speed at which you can develop quality learning events. With a checklist, there is no need to reinvent a list of activities each time you start a new development project and less chance that you will forget a key activity.

On the dark side, development methods offer a temptation to follow a method blindly, which can actually add time to your project. This is a common problem for novice developers. As you read in the beginning of this chapter, only plan activities if you can clearly explain *why* they are needed. Do not let a standard approach limit your flexibility. Every business problem is unique, and each learning need is different. It is extremely important to learn to maintain a repeatable but flexible approach to development in order to meet the needs of the business.

Summary

In this chapter, you read about how to choose activities to create your initial project plan. The Learner First Approach provides you with a repeatable but flexible approach to creating an optimized project plan. Practice applying this approach yourself in the next section.

Practical Exercise

Here is a chance for you to practice determining the appropriate activities for your learning event development. At this point in the development of your project, you should have your project charter and a high-level project plan.

Exercise 4.1. Apply The Learner First Approach.

Referring to the critical path you created for your own project in exercise 3.3, use this worksheet to add detail. After you answer the questions, review your initial project plan (critical path) to see whether you need to add or lengthen any activities. If you need to jog your memory for any topic, refer back to that section earlier in this chapter.

Learner First Worksheet

Define the audience:

_____

_____

_____

_____

Define the skills:

_____

_____

_____

_____

Create learning objectives:

_____

_____

_____

_____

Create skills practice:

_____

_____

_____

_____

Build support material:

_____

_____

_____

_____

Chapter 5

Managing the Project

> *Q:* How does a project get to be three years
> late? (with a nod to Frederik Brooks...)
>
> *A:* One day at a time.

In this chapter, you will learn how to do the following:

- Determine the tasks that need to be completed by the project manager and those that should be completed by a developer

- Monitor the project charter to document business objectives, learning objectives, scope, risk, and constraints

- Monitor the project plan for new course development, course acquisition, or contracted training project

- Adjust critical path networks and bar charts with actual status results in order to manage the project schedule and resource allocation

- Manage the cost of training projects.

In chapter 3, you learned how to create a detailed project plan that included a list of finalized objectives, a chart of project activities, activity dependencies, people assigned to each resource, and how long each activity would take. You learned the difference between duration and elapsed time, and the difference between activity dependency and task dependency. In chapter 4, you learned how to choose the right activities for a course development project. Now it is time for the project to begin—your project plan will be your map. Later, in chapter 7, you will read about activities for a performance consulting project.

Unfortunately, the minute the project begins, your map is out of date. In chapter 3 you learned the importance of "flexible structure." Your project plan will change often, probably immediately. Many of the deliverables that your customer thought it wanted during the planning steps will have changed by the time the activities begin. Changes may include new activities, removed activities, or changed resources, but the most common change will be that the time estimates are now too short. Scope, money, and quality constraints may change as well. In this chapter, you will learn how to manage normal, but inevitable, change.

Philosophically, it is important to constantly remind yourself that a change to the project plan is not a failure on your part. It is impossible to completely anticipate all the events that are going to occur in a project before you get into the nitty-gritty. It is also impossible to freeze the customers' needs, because business change is occurring at all times. Keep yourself from getting too attached to the project plan; if you can't embrace change, at least be prepared to roll with it.

This is not to say that you will make every change requested of you. The focus needs to remain squarely on the project stakeholders who have requested that the learning objectives be met in order to meet the business objectives. This is a crucial point—it is not *your* project, it is *their* project. You are the manager of their request. They make the decision as to when to change the plan to reflect a new need, and you implement the changes. Project managers trying to fight the needs of the business as it changes spend a great deal of energy on angst. To communicate effectively about the trade-offs, in this chapter you'll learn to do the following:

- Establish monitoring criteria
- Manage change
- Troubleshoot.

Dealing with project change involves two steps: identifying the change and managing the change in an effective way. Establishing monitoring criteria is how you measure progress. Again, as in chapter 3, a budget worksheet such as that shown in figure 5.1 will be of the utmost help to you.

Establish Monitoring Criteria

In chapter 2, you read about creating a project charter. This section describes how to build the monitoring criteria from the documents that make up the project definition, including the risk assessment, risk-scenario planning, and constraint prioritization documents. In addition, monitoring

Figure 5.1. Sample project budget worksheet.

Budget Worksheet

Expense Item	Projected Cost	Actual Cost
Labor		
• People		
• Contractors		
• Vendors		
Environment		
• Work space		
• Supplies		
• Computer equipment		
• Software		
• Services		
Process		
• Books		
• Methodology		
• Training		
Organization		
• Meeting expenses		
• Conference calls		
• Travel		
• Room rental		
• Refreshments		
Other		
•		
•		
•		
•		

criteria are derived from the project plan created in chapter 3, including the schedule and the budget worksheet. Each of these components must be monitored to enable a flexible structure for the project.

Risk

Recall the fictional case example presented at the beginning of the book (the fictional one-hour, instructor-led workshop on how to plan and hold a meeting). The risk for the project was a 2.4. The workshop requirements are the riskiest part of a project because they define what the content of the workshop will be.

A list of anticipated risk factors is part of a risk-scenario document. The project manager must remain vigilant in looking for signs that these risk factors are actually coming to fruition. Some of the signs that might indicate trouble along this front are

- new customers with different favorite approaches;
- a "we must build it here" attitude from the customer, which prohibits research or external help;
- a "we must get it outside" attitude from the customer, which prohibits flexibility or creativity; and
- reluctance to attend analysis meetings.

Recall how the risks were prioritized in the meeting management case. One of the high-impact risk factors was the situation in which the key business sponsor left. This is always a serious event because without sponsorship, the project will flounder. As a project manager, you keep your ear to the ground by doing the following:

- Meet regularly with the sponsor.
- Listen for rumors of reorganizations and ask the sponsor directly for clarification.
- Search for backup sponsorship as a contingency plan.

Constraints

Another part of the project definition was prioritizing the constraints of the project. Recall that only one constraint—time, cost, or quality—can be the top priority of a project at any given point it time, although over time, these priorities can and do change.

For an example of how constraints can shift, think back to the fictional case example from the beginning of the book. The order of constraints that the customer agreed to during the define phase was quality, time, then cost. The project plan reflects the importance of having a high-quality product, so many checkpoints, reviews, and walk-throughs are scheduled. Sending multiple customers and multiple developers to those meetings will take time and will have a significant labor cost, but according to the priority of the constraints, that is an acceptable trade-off.

However, what if on the first day of the project, at the first analysis meeting, none of the customers show up? As you call them to see what's going on, they each tell you that they are too busy with business issues to participate in the analysis meetings. However, they would like to be involved in the final (not the preliminary) walk-through of the finished workshop, so that they can offer suggestions. Obviously, it is going to be impossible to deliver a quality product in a timely fashion without customer involvement. What do you do?

You call all the customers and stakeholders and ask for a quick one-hour status meeting. At this meeting you tell them that you have stopped the project until they are available for the analysis meetings. You revisit the constraints and explain that if quality is truly the top priority (which also should be supported by business objectives that were jointly created in the define phase), then you need participation all the way through. Anyone who does not participate in the beginning will not be permitted to critique during the walk-throughs because of the second constraint, which is time. If new voices show up at the end of development, then the project will be forced back into a new needs analysis phase, which will seriously extend the timeline. Since cost is the lowest constraint, you suggest the following alternatives:

- Stop the project until involvement is possible.

- Dedicate a single customer to the course development process. This person will represent the views of others (which is their responsibility, not the project team's) and will be the only one at the walk-throughs as well.

- Hire some temporary help to free up the customers so they can participate (spend money to "buy" quality).

PROJECT MANAGEMENT FOR TRAINERS

- Change the scope of the project so that quality is maintained for a smaller piece, reducing some time and cost of involvement.
- Change the constraints and the project plan.

If these options do not work for the customer, then the behavior tells you that the constraints are not correctly prioritized. If the customers are unwilling or unable to spend time or money, as the above behavior indicates, then quality is not the first constraint. At this point it is important to revisit the constraints diagram and come to an agreement consistent with current behaviors.

Case Example A customer recently had a highly time-constrained course development need and agreed during the define phase that the scope would be narrow in order to meet the cost and time constraints (the second and third constraints, respectively). There was immediate difficulty getting the correct people to meetings. At the first walk-through, the customer began to redesign exercises, critique each page of the book, add other scope, and get deeply into course design. The project manager had to return to the constraints and ask the customer to make a choice: Was time truly the first priority, or was quality? Certainly, she was willing to deliver either, but the schedule and cost of the two approaches was significantly different. Contrary to popular business behavior, you cannot produce a quality-oriented project at a cost-constrained price. In other words, you can't have everything for nothing.

The scope is managed through a scope diagram, which you practiced creating in chapter 2. As the scope changes, the diagram must be updated.

Schedule

Time is monitored through the critical path diagram and Gantt chart. In most project management software packages, there is a way to enter both planned and actual times for each activity. This distinction is important if you are going to use the software to help you monitor the project.

If you use project management software, carefully check it to see how it handles actual and planned activity times. As a project manager, you want to look forward using the planned activity time, but you want to watch for trends and glitches using the actual activity times. The critical path, or longest path of time, which the project manager must monitor carefully, can change as a result of actual time. Figure 5.2 illustrates how this could happen. If you have a fixed due date for a milestone or for the end of the project, which is not unusual, adding actual completion times that extend the project beyond the due date will place every activity on the critical path. When using software, the change becomes obvious because the critical path activities are often color coded in some significant way, such as red. It is a staggering feeling to watch your whole plan "go red" after entering actual completion times.

It is here that the guideline to let the software calculate dates from your activity estimates as much as possible becomes important (see chapter 3). Doing so gives the software more flexibility to reflow the dates when actual activity time is less or greater than planned. Some software packages, however, can treat activities in an unrealistic way once they require more time than the fixed dates allow, including assigning resources to complete 24

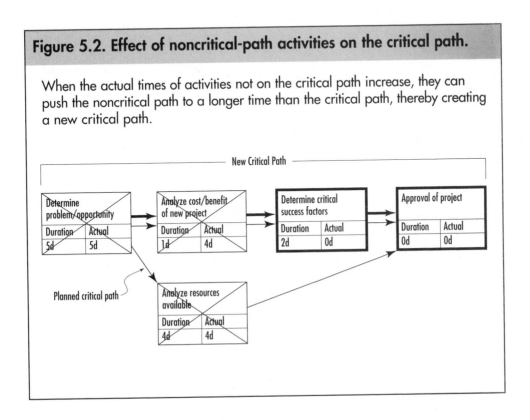

Figure 5.2. Effect of noncritical-path activities on the critical path.

When the actual times of activities not on the critical path increase, they can push the noncritical path to a longer time than the critical path, thereby creating a new critical path.

hours of work in less than a day, or allowing resources to work on 10 activities at the same time. Always view computer-generated charts with a good dose of common sense and watch for unrealistic adjustments.

In some cases, you can toggle between planned and actual views, a feature that can help you compare and learn from history after the project is completed. (See chapter 6 for more information about postproject review.) The danger is that the person using the software may look at the due dates based on planned times but think he or she is seeing the actual times, missing any delays that may have occurred. This mistake is a little harder to make with some of the newer releases of project management software, but you still can miss big problems if you depend exclusively on the software to do your thinking.

Budget

In chapter 3, you learned how to create a budget using a simple worksheet. During the manage phase, the project manager must track the actual costs of the project and compare them with the budget items. Most project management software packages allow you to manage dollars at the activity level, but some people prefer to do the tracking on a simple spreadsheet. Either way, it is important to keep an eye on the costs, watching for the start of insidious trends. The quicker those trends are spotted, the quicker corrective action can be taken.

Manage Change

It is important to point out that the phrase "manage change" is significantly different from the phrase "control change." Misunderstanding the difference between the two is one of the most serious hindrances to project success. If a project manager believes that he or she must control change to be successful, every change will destroy his or her self-confidence, and eventually the project will fail, if only from self-fulfilling expectations. This downward cycle, whereby lowered self-confidence drives failure, which in turn reduces self-confidence, and so forth, occurs in many projects and seems to happen most during times of rapid change. This spiral's effect is not limited to the project manager, and the project team members quickly "catch" the attitude, amplifying the downward spiral.

In contrast, if a project manager often reminds him- or herself that change is going to occur constantly, then he or she is free to react in a thinking way to the changes, rather than in a fearful way. Being open to change is not something that most people do well. Change requires diligence, inner work, assessment, and constant checking of attitude. This principle cannot be overstated—many projects have been destroyed by the project manager's negative attitude toward change. Interestingly, those managers generally do not believe that they are trying to control change; rather, they believe that they are failing to manage well.

Managing change requires a change management plan that is created before project work begins. Change management plans are seen as defensive and distrustful if they are developed out of panic when they are needed. The quickest way to destroy a project is to start building mistrust. Protect yourself and the project by creating a change management process and getting agreement during the end of the plan phase or at the very beginning of the manage phase. Generally, this plan is part of a development approach (discussed in chapters 4 and 7) and is not traditionally thought of as project management. (I mention it here so that you can create the plan if it hasn't been built yet.) It is a document that is essential to the progress of a project, but developers often bypass it in order to avoid conflict with the customer at the start of the project. A change management plan needs to document the following:

- What will happen when the scope appears to change?
- How will the customer and the development team prioritize changes?

A boat metaphor is helpful in understanding how to manage change. A Level 1 change request means that the boat is taking on water but could easily survive with a little bailing. A Level 2 change request means that the boat is taking on enough water that it is starting to sink; it could probably hang in there for a little while, but not indefinitely. The Level 3 change requests are "Titanics," which require immediate attention. If you use this metaphor with your customers, they can call you with their request and let you know the level they perceive it to be. You then can negotiate an agreement with them concerning the level. The developers know the effects of changes on the schedule, cost, and quality of the project, and the customers know the effects of changes on their business. Ultimately, the customer makes the final choice, balancing the trade-offs.

More likely, a change will be stated as something that was in the original requirements. For this reason, the scope diagram created in the define phase is the primary document for determining whether something is truly a change. Scope creep (which creates schedule, budget, and quality slippage) is the most common stress factor in learning event projects. The scope document will never be clear enough to resolve all debates, but it will be a useful tool in the negotiation process.

Troubleshooting (What To Do If You're Behind and It's Your Behind)

This section offers some tips for managing project problems. You *will* have project problems, and something *will* slip. Keep a careful eye on whatever the customer has determined is the third priority of the project—this is almost always the place where there will be pressure to slip. For example, if a customer has agreed that the order of project priorities is time, cost, then scope (quality), you will immediately feel pressure from the customer to add scope without adding time or cost. Determine ahead of time what you will do when that situation occurs.

Time

Time is almost always trouble because it is the easiest to measure. Many projects are given arbitrary due dates simply to have one. Any project date with a 1 in it, like 09/01, is usually arbitrary, especially if those dates fall on a weekend! The first thing to do when you need more time is to challenge the due date.

If you find that things are taking much longer than you had expected, here are some other options:

- Best: Cut the scope of the project and roll out the objectives in phases. Do a great job on a smaller piece, deliver it quickly, and then leverage that success to roll out the rest. Much of the up-front bottlenecks, such as agreeing on terminology, the look of the pages, the exercise flow, and the overall form will be resolved by the smaller, first piece easing the way for the later modules.

  Risk: If the learning is not something you can subdivide and still get the job performance required, quality suffers.

- Might work: Get some money to add resources to the project. Outsource activities that are chewing up lots of time, such as programming or video production. Hire an expert in a skill that your team lacks.

  Risk: Adding people to a project always adds communication time and often can put you further behind. Remember—for every person you add to a project team, you lose 25 percent of everyone else's time to bring that person up to speed.

- Probably won't work: Ask for more time. If time is the first priority, this won't work. If it does, it wasn't really the first priority. It is always a good idea to test the constraints. If it does work, this is the easiest solution.

  Risk: Work expands to fill time.

- Bad idea: Pretend everything is okay. This forces everyone to deliver poor quality, creating piles of rework and distrust.

Cost

Surprisingly, money is a pretty difficult commodity for project managers to measure. If you have hired a lot of outside people to help; have purchased expensive software, hardware, or equipment; or have spent money on "hard" dollar items that are easy to notice, you will get pressure to reduce cost. Internal people costs are somewhat measurable, although the numbers often are artificial. You may get pressure to cut staff to reduce costs. Project development hours themselves are pretty difficult to measure accurately.

Here are some options for cutting costs:

- Best: As previously mentioned, cut the scope of the project, and roll out the learning objectives in phases. Do a great job on a smaller piece, deliver it quickly, and then leverage that success to quickly work on the rest. If people truly are cost conscious, adding phases will be well received.

  Risk: If the learning is not something you can subdivide and still attain the desired level of job performance, quality will suffer.

- Might work: Ask for more time so that the resources that are currently allocated to the project can continue to work on the project.

  Risk: Adding labor time actually adds cost (of hours for the work). Sometimes this is not an issue, depending on how closely hours are accounted for.

- Probably won't work: Ask for more money. If money is the first priority, this won't work. If it does, it wasn't really the first priority, and you will get some money to add resources to the project. Hire an expert in a skill that your team lacks.

  Risk: Adding people to a project always adds communication time and often can get you further behind.

- Bad idea: Pretend everything is okay. This forces everyone to deliver poor quality, creating piles of costly rework.

Quality

Project managers often are emotionally surprised when quality becomes an issue. The customer wants the best and may have many ideas about how to improve the work for which you, as a developer, are the expert. The most important rule is not to let your ego get in your way—which is a difficult thing to do. As developers, we take great pride in our work and want to be appreciated for it. It is a humbling experience to be critiqued by a person outside the field. However, it is vital to remember at all times that the learning event is not your deliverable; it belongs to and is being funded by the customer. They are the ones who judge whether it is good. They are the ones who understand the business context in which it will be implemented. Here are some other thoughts on how to handle quality critique:

- Best: If the change is within the scope, make the change quickly. If the changes start to cycle (changing something back after it was changed to something new, which is not unusual), begin to log all changes so that you can explain to the customer the cost of the constant tuning. If the project has quality as the first constraint, you should be tuning regardless of cost and time. If it is not, inform the customer honestly what the changes are costing him or her in terms of time and cost. Draw a line at what you can change for fixed-bid contracts. As with time changes, cut the scope of the project, and roll out the learning objectives in phases.

  Risk: Negotiating changes is a major factor in the trust between you and your client. It is vital that you are honest about how you feel, both with yourself (difficult) and with your customer (easier, but still difficult).

- Might work: Ask for more time so that personnel who are currently assigned to the project can continue to refine the project.

Risk: Adding labor time can sometimes hurt quality because of the increased communication required.

- Probably won't work: Ask for more money. Money is commonly not useful for buying quality because it adds new people, which adds complexity to a project. It might work if you obtain money to hire an expert in a skill that your team lacks.

   Risk: Adding people to a project always adds communication time and often can get you further behind.

- Bad idea: Pretend everything is okay. This forces everyone to get angry at each other. A project cannot be successful if the customers and the developers are at odds. Avoid this situation at any cost because it creates a negative reinforcing loop that is difficult to break.

History Tells Us . . .

Projects are always unique, always exciting at the beginning, and always terrifying once they start. There is no honeymoon period for a project manager—the glitches begin almost immediately. Keeping the documents created in the define phase close at hand and constantly keeping the lines of communication open between the team and the customers is the only way to drive project success. Post the following nuggets of truth on your wall:

- It's usually time.
- Manage scope to manage quality.
- It is the customer's project, not yours.
- Change is necessary, good, and inevitable.
- You will learn something new in every project, every day.

Summary

In this chapter, you have read about how to manage a project once it begins. To manage a project as it progresses requires the confidence to clearly communicate the truth while listening carefully to the customers' needs. In chapter 6, you will learn how to review a completed project to build your expertise for future projects.

Practical Exercises

Now apply what you've learned in this chapter. Referring to your own project and to the documentation that you created through the exercises in this book, consider the specific solutions to your own project.

Establish Monitoring Criteria

Exercise 5.1. Plan for changes to constraints.

As discussed in this chapter, the third and second constraints will be tested almost immediately.

Thinking about your own project, what are those constraints?

What will you do, specifically, when the testing occurs?

Use the chart below to organize your notes.

Third Constraint: _____

Action: _____

_____

_____

Second Constraint: _____

Action: _____

_____

_____

Exercise 5.2: The schedule.

In this chapter, you learned the effects of actual completion times on the critical path of a project. Create a strategy for updating your critical path diagram by answering the following questions as they relate to your own project:

• Who will be in charge of recording actual completion times?

_____

• Where will they record it?

_____

• How frequently will the information be gathered and entered?

_____

• How frequently will the updated project plans be shared with the project team?

_____

• With the customer?

_____

• What will you do as project manager when the critical path changes?

_____

_____

_____

The answers to these questions may lead you to add activities to your project plan.

Exercise 5.3: Managing change.

Create a strategy and process for dealing with constant change on your own project, both from the customers' and the developers' standpoint.

- What will the ranking of the problems be?

_____

_____

_____

- Define criteria for each; consider the boat metaphor presented in this chapter.

_____

_____

_____

- Who will make the initial determination of the ranking?

_____

- What documentation will be created?

_____

_____

- How will you track the history of change requests?

_____

_____

- How will the final ranking be determined?

_____

_____

Troubleshooting

Exercise 5.4: Time.

In this chapter, you learned some tips for troubleshooting schedule challenges. Using the guidelines in the troubleshooting section, make notes here about what you will do if your schedule is threatened (remember to consider leveraging more money or less scope):

_____

_____

_____

_____

_____

_____

_____

_____

_____

_____

_____

_____

_____

_____

_____

_____

Exercise 5.5: Cost.

In this chapter, you learned some tips for troubleshooting an overshot budget. Using the guidelines in the troubleshooting section, make notes here about what you will do if your funds are cut or prove to be insufficient (again, remember to consider leveraging more money or less scope):

Exercise 5.6: Quality.

In this chapter, you learned some tips for managing quality. Using the guide-lines in the troubleshooting section, make notes here about what you will do if your customer suddenly gets stubborn (from *your* perspective) about changes (remember to consider leveraging more time or more resources):

_____

_____

_____

_____

_____

_____

_____

_____

_____

_____

_____

_____

_____

_____

_____

_____

_____

_____

Chapter 6

Reviewing the Project

Q: **How do we improve organization-wide project management?**

A: **Share project experiences through postproject review.**

In this chapter, you will learn how to perform a postproject review for every project to ensure the knowledge management of project intellectual capital.

In previous chapters you read how to create a project charter in the design phase, create a project plan in the plan phase, and then implement and adjust the project plan in the manage phase. When the project is completed, it is tempting to just move on. As learning experts, you know that learning (which I like to define as a change in behavior) occurs through reflection following mistakes. As project teams move quickly from finished projects to new projects, often no time is taken to reflect on what happened and the ramifications for future project work. The postproject review, discussed in this chapter, holds the key to identifying lessons learned and then, most important, changing the behavior you bring to future project work. It is only through this activity that true project management expertise accumulates in an organization.

Certainly, personal reflection on project work is of great benefit; just thinking about the project on your own can create personal behavior change that will improve your own project work. The true leverage comes, however, through project team reflection. In *The Knowledge-Creating Company: How Japanese Companies Create the Dynamics of Innovation*, by I. Nonaka, H. Takeuchi, and H. Takeuchi (New York: Oxford University Press, 1995), the authors explain the life cycle of knowledge: creation, exchange, transformation, and then recycling to creation. Knowledge management occurs when project teams reflect on their project experiences together, transform that knowledge as their experiences are vocalized and exchanged, and then create new knowledge through action plans for the future. Using a postproject review approach ensures that the life cycle of knowledge continues organizationally.

Unfortunately, little postproject reflection occurs. Statistics gathered over the past 20 years point out that most projects fail to meet their quality, cost, or time goals. Even with advancing technology, new methods, and lots of new research, project teams are still making the same mistakes. These mistakes are reduced only through knowledge management—by identifying them in a postproject review and sharing them with other project teams.

Of course, your project will not be exactly the same as someone else's, and you can be sure that something new will surprise you on every project. All the knowledge from all the previous teams' experiences cannot save you from surprise glitches. But certain events seem to occur in every project, such as scope creep and communication problems. These events will be glaringly obvious during a postproject review. This chapter will provide you with the following tools:

- A sample postproject review template
- A sample process for postproject review
- Information on using systems thinking to review a project.

A Sample Postproject Review Template

The postproject review gathers information about the following "manageables" of a project:

- Time and deadlines
- Costs and budget
- Specifications and learning objectives
- Staffing
- Technology, tools, and techniques

- Performance
- Corrective action
- External suppliers and stakeholders.

If you remember the initial project charter, the three high-level components of risk were size, requirements, and technology. The project priorities documented as constraints were time, cost, and quality. Basically, the postproject review questions debrief across these dimensions. In addition, it is helpful to revisit any scenario planning done as part of the project charter and to reflect on the accuracy of the scenario events brainstormed and the action plans proposed.

Sample Process for Postproject Review

As mentioned at the start of this chapter, even if you are the only one executing it, there is tremendous value in answering the questions of the postproject review (see figure 6.1). Personal reflection creates personal improvement, so your time is well invested. Real organizational learning, however, occurs when the whole project team answers the questions together. Below is a suggested three-step process for efficiently performing this review:

1. Individually reflect on the project using the postproject review questions. (Time needed: less than one hour.)

2. Summarize all the responses in one document, without using names, for review by all team members. (Time needed for summarization, two hours; for review, less than one hour.)

3. Spend half a day with the entire team covering the following agenda:

   - Create a list of the top 10 lessons learned based on the responses to the review questions and any new thoughts.

   - Create a list of helpful hints for future projects.

   - Plan a strategy for sharing this information with future project teams (include the project charter information so the context of the project is clearly understood.)

If possible, get a neutral facilitator to manage the face-to-face meeting. Project managers often are tempted to perform this function themselves, but they are too close to the issues to do a fair job. Since it may be difficult to get funding (especially when the project is already over budget) for a facilitator, you may be able to borrow a facilitator from another project with

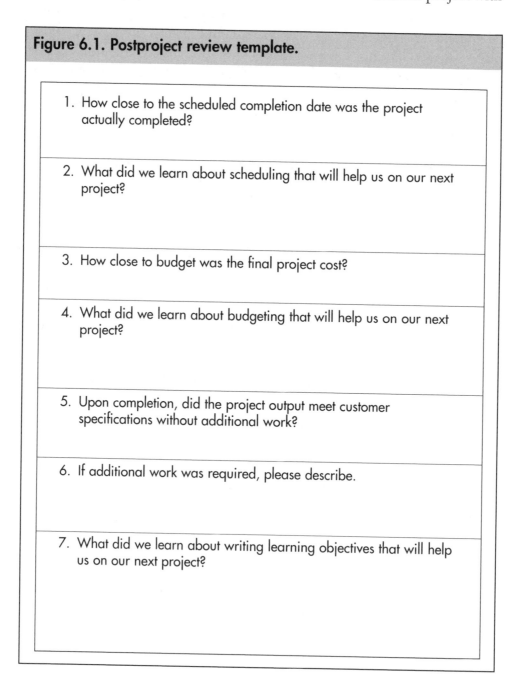

Figure 6.1. Postproject review template.

1. How close to the scheduled completion date was the project actually completed?

2. What did we learn about scheduling that will help us on our next project?

3. How close to budget was the final project cost?

4. What did we learn about budgeting that will help us on our next project?

5. Upon completion, did the project output meet customer specifications without additional work?

6. If additional work was required, please describe.

7. What did we learn about writing learning objectives that will help us on our next project?

8. What did we learn about staffing that will help us on our next project?

9. What did we learn about monitoring performance that will help us on our next project?

10. What did we learn about constraints that will help us on our next project?

11. What techniques were developed that will be useful on our next project?

12. What recommendations do we have for future research prior to a project?

13. What lessons did we learn from our dealings with outside contractors?

14. If we had the opportunity to do the project over, what would we do differently?

15. What would we do the same?

the promise of helpful hints for improving his or her own project management capabilities.

Using Systems Thinking to Review a Project

For projects that were either very important, very problematic, or just very different, teams should spend a little more time capturing the lessons learned using a Learning Organization technique called *systems thinking*. Systems thinking is a group technique that creates a visual model which depicts, through cause-and-effect loops, the different events that influenced the success of a project. (See Peter Senge's book *The Fifth Discipline* [New York: Doubleday, 1994] for more information on systems thinking and Learning Organization techniques.)

Figure 6.2 shows a simple example of a model that answers the question "Why did this project struggle?"

Systems thinking must always start with a "why" question that indicates the depth of the analysis that will be done. If the team cannot come up with a single why question, it will not be able to talk coherently about causes and effects. When at a loss, it is always effective to just start with the question "Why did this project struggle?" and let the true question evolve as the team proceeds.

If you read figure 6.2 several times, you will notice that one mistake can trigger a negative cycle of increasing mistakes. However, if any of the variables can be flipped in the other direction (that is, decreased), all the others will follow. For example, if you decrease *perceived workload*, the other variables will decrease as well, starting a positive cycle of fewer mistakes and reduced workload.

A second, long-term cause and effect exists between *mistakes* and *project work volume*. If mistakes continue to escalate over time, the project will be given less and less responsibility and the customer will look for ways to avoid this team. As mistakes increase, project work volume decreases over the long term. Essentially, the story of this loop is that mistakes foster more mistakes and that if the situation continues, the team will lose the project. The loop to the right in figure 6.2 is another reinforcing loop with the same net effect—the mistakes foster mistakes, and the project situation worsens.

Figure 6.2. An example of a simple systems thinking model that answers the question "Why did this project struggle?"

Internal, or endogenous, variables appear in boxes; external, or exogenous, variables appear in shaded cubes. *s* means "same"—as one variable increases, the affected variable increases as well. Likewise, *o* means "opposite"—as one variable increases, the affected variable decreases.

To read the model, begin with the variable *mistakes*. Moving through the loop on the left ("You broke it, you fix it"), as mistakes increase, *project work volume* increases. As project work volume increases, eventually the team notices, so *perceived workload* increases. External to the project, *metrics* (measurements), *inadequate training,* and *job resources* also influence the project workload. As the perceived workload increases, *stress* increases. As stress increases, mistakes increase and the cycle repeats itself.

The loop to the right ("I'm mad, you're mad") gets to the heart of the customer's perception. As mistakes increase, the *client's trust in the project* decreases (indicated by *o*). As this trust decreases, the *client's anger* increases. At the same time, external factors, such as *inadequate training, job resources,* and *bad systems* (software) may also influence the client's anger. As the client's anger increases, stress (on the project team) increases, which in turn increases mistakes.

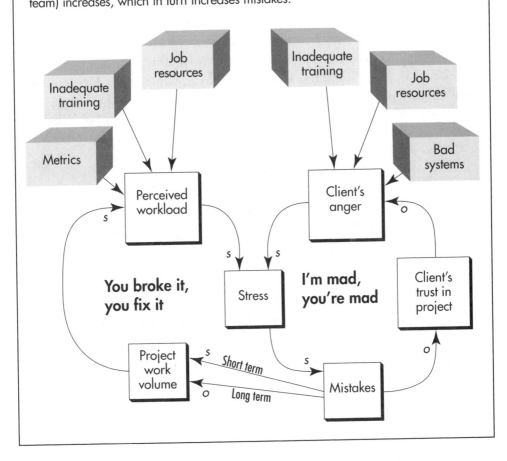

The most important learning from this type of analysis is to determine an appropriate intervention. In this case, a proposed solution must include intervention for both loops. If only one loop is "fixed," the remaining negative loop will force it back to its original negative cycle. In addition, any variable that can be decreased will have the net effect of influencing both loops, because they always share variables. However, this effort will have to be constant because the external factors will always work to push the loop back into a negative cycle. Some examples for specific interventions are as follows:

- Help project team members deal better with stress.

- Teach project team members how to triage mistakes so they don't always add to the project workload.

- Teach project team members how to narrow the scope when mistakes force the project workload to unrealistic levels.

- Manage the customer relationship and customer expectations as a primary success factor.

Creating systems models is best done with an experienced systems thinking facilitator. The analysis can generally be performed in a day, with an additional day to determine the interventions for future projects. I do not recommend that you hand the model, without explanation, to future project teams. However, the loop "stories" and the proposed interventions are meaningful when they come from people who experienced it themselves.

History Tells Us . . .

All projects have struggles, and looking back at a struggle is no reflection of the inadequacy of any member of a project team. The teams that can look back and learn from struggles will be much more successful in the future than teams that hide from these lessons. The postproject review allows a team and an organization to do the following:

- Build knowledge about success factors of projects for their business

- Create a team consensus that leaves the participants on an open and forward-thinking note, rather than hiding from an inadequate project result. This consensus builds bridges for future project teamwork.

- Create a building block for implementing knowledge management in a pragmatic manner so that knowledge can be created, exchanged, and transformed for measurable business return.

Summary

In this chapter, you read about how to review a learning event project once it ends. To review a project requires honest reflection and sharing. Denial is not healthy when project management improvement is the goal. Now practice the review-phase activities using your own experience.

Practical Exercise

Exercise 6.1. Postproject review.

Complete the postproject review template for a project you have worked on by answering each of the questions in the template. Find one other person who was involved with that project, and ask him or her to reflect on the project, following the template as much as possible, and to share his or her answers with you.

What did you learn about project management?

_____

_____

_____

What would you do differently?

_____

_____

_____

What would you do the same way?

_____

_____

_____

Write your lessons learned in the space provided.

_____

_____

_____

_____

Postproject review template.

1. How close to the scheduled completion date was the project actually completed?

2. What did we learn about scheduling that will help us on our next project?

3. How close to budget was the final project cost?

4. What did we learn about budgeting that will help us on our next project?

5. Upon completion, did the project output meet customer specifications without additional work?

6. If additional work was required, please describe.

7. What did we learn about writing learning objectives that will help us on our next project?

8. What did we learn about staffing that will help us on our next project?

(continued next page)

Exercise 6.1. *(continued)*

---

9. What did we learn about monitoring performance that will help us on our next project?

---

10. What did we learn about constraints that will help us on our next project?

---

11. What techniques were developed that will be useful on our next project?

---

12. What recommendations do we have for future research prior to a project?

---

13. What lessons did we learn from our dealings with outside contractors?

---

14. If we had the opportunity to do the project over, what would we do differently?

---

15. What would we do the same?

Chapter 7

Managing Performance Consulting Projects

Q: **How can I manage the new consulting responsibilities called performance consulting?**

A: **Manage a flexible, repeatable process for consulting.**

In this chapter, you will learn how to do the following:

- Determine the tasks that need to be done by the project manager and those that should be done by a developer

- Build a project charter to document business objectives, learning objectives, scope, risk, and constraints

- Choose appropriate activities to manage for a performance consulting effort.

Performance consulting is all the rage in the human resources (HR) field and in most training organizations. Like other departments, a corporate HR department must prove its value to the organization by providing a measurable return-on-investment. Many human resource activities, including workshops, have been wrongly thrown at performance problems and have not solved the complete problem—or worse, solved no problems at all.

But moving from the role of a trainer, developer, or facilitator to that of a consultant is not an easy task. Consulting work requires a different set of skills, including the ability to facilitate, negotiate, manage conflict, solve problems, and listen. In chapter 4, you learned about an approach to course development called The Learner First Approach and the activities that have to be managed in developing a learning event. Similarly, the skills required for project management and development are essential components of consulting; the process is different, but the core competencies are similar.

If anything, the time pressures of performance consulting are more extreme. When a supervisor is looking for help with a performance problem, there is not a lot of tolerance for analysis time. Performance consultants must be able to move quickly through, but not neglect, an analysis of the problem, and then partner with the customer to create a solution. Trust your instincts and your experiences. You will often see situations that you have seen before. Try not to jump to a solution, however, and learn how to ask the right questions to make sure you are heading to the right conclusion.

The notion of planning a project implies that you know you are doing the right project in the first place. A verbal request is not always enough to trigger a consulting project. If the project charter cannot be completed, the performance consulting project must never begin. You must have a thorough understanding of the client's business need.

This chapter describes a method for performance consulting for any size situation. You will learn about the following techniques:

- Creating a rational plan
- Working back from the date.

A Rational Plan

Figure 7.1 shows a model for approaching consulting. The PACT Model ("Make a PACT with your business customer") ensures that

- appropriate analysis of the problem occurs before the solution is created,
- ownership of the performance improvement remains with the business customer through partnering, and
- external and internal work is carefully balanced for effectiveness.

Step 1: Plan

The *plan* phase of the PACT model overlaps a great deal with the define phase of The Dare Approach. Notice that the only significant difference is that you create performance objectives instead of learning objectives, although the approach is similar. (Refer back to chapter 2 for more information about creating objectives; the important points to remember are the ABCs of objectives: audience, behavior, and condition.)

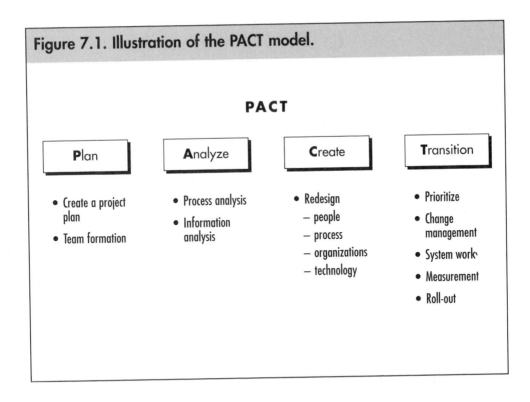

Figure 7.1. Illustration of the PACT model.

The performance objectives are important because after a solution has been implemented, they will be the criteria used to measure the success of the initiative. The solution may contain one or many activities, such as training, process redesign, reward structure redesign, and organizational design. Individually, each activity often will not be sufficient to improve performance, but implemented together, they create a systemic approach to meeting the performance goals. It is vital that the performance objectives be clearly measurable and agreed to by the client (for example, "After the performance improvement project, the sales staff will increases sales of our new line by 15 percent in the first year.").

Step 2: Analyze

This is the phase in which the initial detective work is done. Just like in The Learner First Approach, a careful analysis must be done to ensure that symptoms are mapped correctly to problem causes. Without that, the wrong problem might be tackled. Consider the following questions that must be answered:

- What is the perceived performance gap?
- What would the performance look like if it were improved? How would one measure that improvement?
- What are the people issues that are preventing improved performance?
- What are the organizational issues, including reward and appraisal processes, that are preventing improved performance?
- What are the technology issues preventing improved performance?

A good way to gather this information is through a combination of group and individual interviews. Here is a sequence that works well and quickly:

1. Distribute a letter from the budget client to all the stakeholders explaining the goal of the project. Request that the managers attend a one-hour initial data-gathering session. Distribute with this letter the questions to be discussed so that participants have time to think about responses.

2. Hold the one-hour meeting and discuss the answers to the questions through standard facilitation techniques. You will not get much good data here, but you will quickly see where the power in the organization lies by the behavior of this group. Explain to this group the problem being addressed, and ask them to sign up their staff and themselves for a 20-minute, one-on-one interview during a three- to five-day period a few weeks later. I call these the "doctor is in" sessions.

3. Invite the secretaries of the organization to lunch, and ask them the same questions. Secretaries know everything, so you will get good information from them. Treating them with respect by buying them lunch will upset the status quo and will help motivate people to get to the 20-minute interviews just to find out what is going on.

4. Hold a one-hour group meeting for the executive management similar to the one held for the managers. Again, note the behavior in the room to better understand the power base.

5. Schedule phone calls or visits (if possible) with some key customers to hear their perception of the issues.

6. Hold the "doctor is in" sessions.

These are some of the activities that would make up the project plan for the analyze step. As you gather this information, it is essential that you remain neutral. As you hear from more and more people, you must fight the urge to jump to conclusions or pick sides. It is important to capture all the information and synthesize it so that all views are represented. As the final results are published, create a table rating each issue's importance, according to the number of people whom you have heard express each issue.

Clearly, the only way to be effective at an undertaking of this magnitude is by careful project management. To remind yourself about how to estimate, schedule these interviews, and track their status, review chapter 3. In estimating, be sure to consider the people working on each activity, the amount of communication required by the project, and the overhead of the business culture.

Step 3: Create

In the *create* phase, the clearer understanding of the problem is translated into a solution design. The performance consultant *must* facilitate this process with the people who will be responsible for implementing that solution. New processes and strategies created exclusively by a consultant are rarely, if ever, successful. For ownership to occur, the people affected must be actively involved.

As you begin to work with these groups (or task forces), scheduling and time commitment become a huge problem. Again, it is important to manage this work as specified in chapter 5. Surprise glitches and delays are common when you are working on projects like these, especially when analysis is threatening to some of the stakeholders.

Step 4: Transition

Although many people like to think that a performance consulting project is finished once the solution has been implemented, that is never the case. The transition to the new solution is the toughest part of the project. It is here that all the underground currents of fear and anxiety surface to become weapons of destruction. A project manager must be vigilant at this time to keep the project moving forward, although sometimes it will feel more like you are keeping it from sliding backward. The project charter created as part of the define phase, along with the project plan created in the plan phase, will be the defense you need to remind people of the original vision and keep the project on track.

Working Back From the Due Date

Most performance consulting projects start with a fixed due date. People who have admitted to problems do not have a lot of time to wait for a solution. Even if the problems have existed for months or even years, understanding the magnitude of the problem because of your analysis work accelerates the desire for resolution.

So, in the real world (versus the world in project management books), you don't have unlimited time and resources to finish a project, especially a performance consulting project. Instead, you have to work backward and use the time you have. To manage this frustrating reality, here is an algorithm that is based on the PACT phases:

Plan	10 percent
Analyze	40 percent
Create	30 percent
Transition	20 percent

This breakdown makes it a little easier to allocate the amount of time you have for each phase. For example, if you have been given six calendar months to finish a project (which is roughly 120 working days), the work breaks down like this:

Plan	12 days (2.5 business weeks)
Analyze	48 days (10 business weeks)
Create	36 days (7.5 business weeks)
Transition	24 days (5 business weeks)

Remember, this breakdown is based on elapsed time, *not* duration (refer to chapter 3 for a discussion of the difference between the two).

Another word of warning: It will be tempting to rush to create as fast as possible, shortchanging the plan and analyze phase. At first, skimping on planning and analyzing will seem to buy you a lot of time to get the "important" work done. Ultimately, however, you will end up creating a solution that is based on an incomplete understanding of the problem, or worse, you will create the wrong solution entirely. This will become painfully evident when you hit the transition phase and everything blows up. At this point, you will be forced to return and analyze after the fact, and it will probably take much longer because of stress and time pressures on both the consultant and the client. This pattern constantly repeats itself in projects, and it is so insidious that even experienced project managers fall victim time and time again.

Summary

In this chapter, you have read about how to apply the same project management techniques that enable you to develop learning events to performance consulting work. Performance consulting resembles learning event development, but it has some fundamental differences. Table 7.1 summarizes the information presented in the chapter.

Like learning event development, performance consulting engagements are not easy. No silver bullet will effectively destroy all the problems that may occur. The best defense is to carefully plan and manage the project through flexible, yet structured, project management.

Table 7.1. Summary of the Differences Between Learning Event Development and Project Consulting

Characteristic	Similarity Between Learning Event Development and PC	Difference Between Learning Event Development and PC
Creeping scope	Pressure in both	More pressure in PC work
High political risk	Some learning events	All PC work
Difficult to schedule	Limited difficulty in learning events	Multiple schedules conflict in PC work, usually more clients
Stakeholder push back	Limited in learning events	Frequent in PC work
Time constrained	Somewhat in learning events	Highly constrained in PC work

Practical Exercise

Below is a scenario for a performance consulting engagement. Apply the steps from the plan and define phases of The Dare Approach to this scenario as well as the activities of the PACT model that you read about in this chapter. The purpose of the exercise is to plan a performance consulting project to see the difference between it and a course development project.

Exercise 7.1: Some Practice for performance consulting project management.

You are part of the HR department at a large utility company. You have been called in to talk to the employees of a new subsidary, Power Surge, that your company has been developing in an attempt to have a more diversified business when deregulation hits in a few years. This subsidiary has been marketing surge protection devices to existing customers for more than a year. Sales have not grown as quickly as the company had hoped, and the CEO has asked you to go in, look things over, and report back about what should be done. He confides in you that he suspects that the salespeople need training, but is interested in hearing what you find out. He agrees that you will need to interview all the employees in the organization, which include one president, two vice presidents, a manager and four staff in the sales department, a manager and three staff in accounting, and a manager and five staff in technical support. Information technology support, human resources (including training), and marketing development are currently "bought" from the parent company through charge-back. The CEO must have your answer in one month because he must make a recommendation to the board about the viability of this subsidiary at the company's annual board meeting a month and a half from now.

You will not be responsible for implementing any of your recommendations, but you must propose a business case for the solution. You will not have anyone else helping you with this project, and you will be dedicated to it full time between now and then. Consider the following:

- What are the business objectives?
- What are the performance objectives?
- What is the scope of this project?
- What is the risk?
- What are the constraints?

Here are some sample answers—your responses may differ.

Business objective: The final report will allow the parent company to accurately invest in the Power Surge subsidiary to obtain the best return on that investment.

Performance objective: This project will provide the answers to the following questions:

- What is preventing the growth of the Power Surge subsidiary, according to the people in the organization and some of its customers?

- Is it a good investment strategy for the parent company to continue to invest in this venture? If yes, what types of investments should be made?

Consider what activities should be planned. Here are some sample activities:

- Create an initial letter that will introduce the project from the CEO. Distribute to everyone in the organization with an invitation to the meetings that will be held.

- Create the project charter.

- Schedule a one-hour meeting with the three middle managers.

- Hold the one-hour manager meeting.

- Follow up with meeting notes and the "doctor is in" schedule after the manager meeting.

- Schedule a lunch meeting with the two administrative assistants.

- Hold the lunch meeting.

- Follow up with specific logistical needs for the "doctor is in" meetings.

- Schedule the "doctor is in" meetings.

- Hold the "doctor is in" meetings.

- Schedule three key customer meetings (phone or live).

- Hold three key customer meetings.

- Follow up with notes from key customer meetings and thank-you letters.

- Schedule a meeting with key contacts in IT, HR, and marketing.

- Hold the meeting with IT, HR, and marketing.

- Follow up with notes from IT, HR, and marketing meetings and thank-you letters.

(continued next page)

Exercise 7.1: *(continued)*

- Synthesize results.

- Create document of existing situation.

- Create prioritized table of proposed solution sets.

- Do rough cost-benefit analysis for each proposed solution.

Think about the activities that you will need to do, then create a critical path network and Gantt chart:

- What activities will you need to do to deliver a report in one month?

- How long will each activity take?

- What will the schedule look like?

Figure 7.2 shows a sample scope diagram for this project. In this case, a critical path network is not necessary because only one person is working on all the activities, meaning that there is only one project path. A timeline or Gantt chart would be more useful.

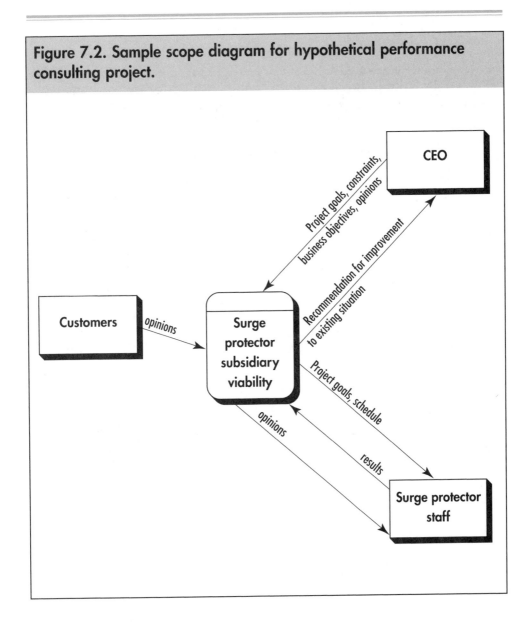

Figure 7.2. Sample scope diagram for hypothetical performance consulting project.

Figure 7.3 is an example of the time allocated for the above activities according to the PACT model algorithm, working back from the due date. Figure 7.4 is a worksheet showing the amount of risk involved in this project according to the formula described in chapter 2.

(continued next page)

Exercise 7.1: *(continued)*

Figure 7.3. Sample breakdown of time allocated for performance consulting activities according to the PACT model algorithm.

Allocation of Time for Power Surge Project

Schedule: Assumes 20 days to complete project, or one month		
Plan	2 days	Create the project charter.
Analyze	10 days	All interviews and meetings scheduled, held, and followed up within two weeks. "Doctor is in" will require two full days.
Create	8 days	Includes synthesis as well as production and design of document.
Transition	n/a	4 days here spread between analyze and create.

Figure 7.4. Worksheet showing the amount of risk involved in this project.

Each category is given a risk value of 1 to 10, with 10 representing the highest amount of risk.

Risk Assessment for Power Surge Project

Element	Rating
Size	5
Structure	8
Technology	1
Average	4.3=medium risk to business High political and career risk to you

Chapter 8

A Template for Managing External Suppliers

Q: How can I effectively outsource learning development and delivery?

A: Follow a flexible, repeatable process for managing vendors.

This chapter will show you how to do the following:

- Determine the tasks that need to be done by the project manager and those that should be done by a developer (in this case, an external vendor).
- Build a project charter to document business objectives, learning objectives, scope, risk, and constraints.
- Build a project plan for a new course development, course acquisition, or contracted training project.
- Create a work breakdown structure to uncover the activities needed to complete a project.
- Plan and manage the cost of training projects.
- Create critical path networks and bar charts to manage the project schedule and resource allocation.
- Accurately estimate work effort for a project.
- Perform a postproject review for every project to ensure the management of project intellectual capital.

In many training organizations, the staff is lean and limited resources are available; most of these are dedicated to administration of the learning events. Like many consultants, you may find yourself in a situation where you must contract out your development and delivery work. Managing a project that will be delivered through an external vendor carries with it its own unique challenges, so the project must still be managed carefully. Some people make the mistake of believing that once you contract out work, you never have to think about it again. In the best case, outsourcing means that 60 percent of the work will be done externally, but 40 percent of the work is so dependent on the expertise within the company that it can never be done outside. Outsourcing requires internal resource time and coordination but, if it is done correctly, not as much time as doing the entire project internally.

This chapter offers tips for managing external vendors, whether for a large learning event development project or simply the presentation of one workshop. You will learn about the following elements of dealing with contractors:

- The secret to success
- Define: detail vs. flexibility
- Contractor law
- Confidentiality
- Establishing communication standards
- Change management
- Knowledge transfer
- Shared risk.

The Secret to Success

"He no longer trusts you because you insist on telling him the truth about his project." I overheard this strange statement from an internal person to the vendor of outsourced work. As the quotation illustrates, the secret to success with managing external vendors is not about a detailed, unbreakable contract. Rather, it is about the quality of communication. People make an outsourcing relationship work through frequent, clear communication that is filled with integrity. The core capacity that drives the effectiveness of communication is trust. Figure 8.1 shows a model that explains this dynamic using a causal loop diagram (a technique used to document systems thinking) that you saw in chapter 6.

Figure 8.1. Causal loop diagram illustrating the ideal communication dynamic with outside suppliers.

As the supplier's trust in the internal contact increases, he or she is more open and honest in communicating with the internal contact because fear of retribution is diminished. The small s indicates that as trust by the supplier increases, open and honest communication goes the same way—it increases (indicated by the s).

In the second loop, increasing performance reconfirms the internal contact's choice of the supplier. This builds the internal contact's trust in the supplier and in turn allows the internal contact to be more open and honest in communicating.

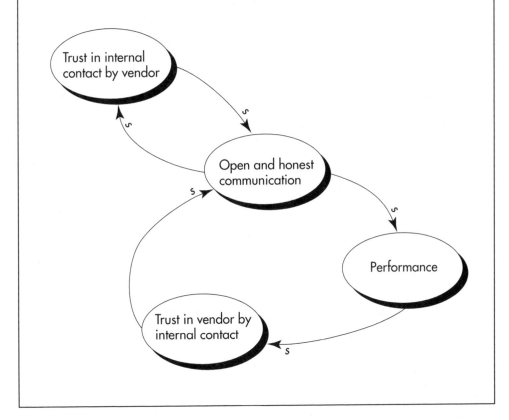

As a vendor's trust in the internal contact increases, he or she becomes more open and honest in communicating with the internal contact because fear of retribution is diminished. As communication between the vendor and the internal contact becomes more open and honest, performance increases. The vendor and internal contact thus are able to move forward with a shared vision toward the goals of the business. In addition, they do not have to spend quite so much time covering their tracks or protecting their backside. Efforts then are expended more effectively toward the goals of the project.

This type of loop is called a *reinforcing loop*, which means that the situation reinforces itself. You are probably familiar with the expression "we seem to be in a negative reinforcing loop." When reinforcing loops are working well, the situation—in this case, project work—just gets better and better; but when trouble hits, things get worse and worse.

The danger of reinforcing loops is that if any one variable starts to degrade, the rest will follow suit. For example, let's suppose that one day there is a project glitch—perhaps the vendor misses a key milestone or the quality of the performance is not acceptable. As performance decreases, the internal contact's trust in the vendor goes the same way—it decreases. As trust in the vendor decreases, open and honest communication starts to degrade, which in turn degrades the vendor's trust in the internal contact. Now the relationship is spiraling downward.

Hope is not lost. Although reinforcing loops are susceptible to a decrease in any one variable, they can be improved by increasing any one variable. In this case, the best intervention is to model open and honest communication at all times, regardless of the level of trust. This openness will eventually create trust if you hang in there long enough. Of course, the assumption here is that you only work with honest suppliers. Clearly, you can't make yourself trust someone, but you can behave as though you do. The next section looks at the relationship between contracts and trust.

RFPs: Detail vs. Flexibility

When training departments decide that they are going to outsource some or all of their services, the first step is usually to create a Request for Proposal (RFP). The RFP provides the suppliers interested in the business with a list of the requirements for the project and may provide the evaluation criteria that will be used to compare supplier proposals. Suppliers then prepare proposals to sell their services. This can be a tedious and time-consuming undertaking, but it can help ensure that the best match is found.

Two types of RFPs create a trust problem right from the start: *detailed* and *vague* (see figure 8.2). Before the supplier is even chosen, the RFP can set up a negative reinforcing loop.

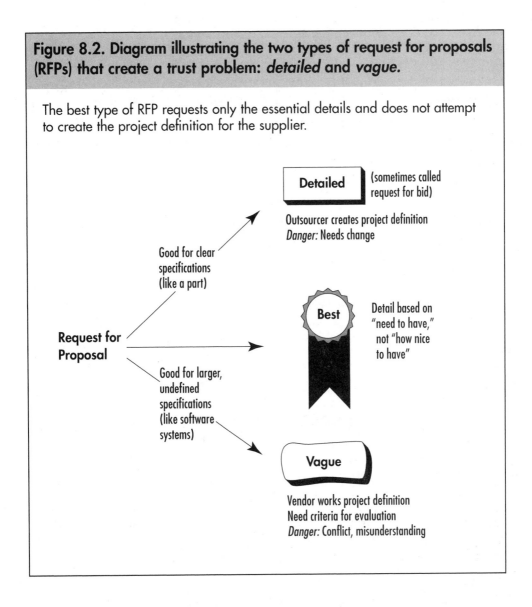

Figure 8.2. Diagram illustrating the two types of request for proposals (RFPs) that create a trust problem: *detailed* **and** *vague.*

The best type of RFP requests only the essential details and does not attempt to create the project definition for the supplier.

The detailed RFP (often called a request for bid) contains every scrap of information that will be needed. Every detail of every activity is specified, and measurements are defined. In a sense, the detailed RFP contains the project definition (see chapter 2, the design phase), the project plan (see chapter 3, the plan phase) and the project review criteria. In some cases, the detailed RFP also may attempt to quantify the manage phase. The belief behind this type of RFP is that it protects the business from being "ripped off." Clearly such RFPs are written on the basis of a lack of trust right from the start.

The lack of trust flows through to the response from the supplier, whose proposal will contain massive generalities wordsmithed to look like detail. Quantity will replace quality in the hope that the poundage of the proposal will serve as proof of its merit. Savvy, unethical suppliers know how to leave loopholes in this type of proposal so that the customer will not be able to catch them padding the hours or dollars. The bigger the proposal, the less likely it will be read carefully. Again, the lack of trust becomes contagious; across an industry, this behavior can become status quo.

It is irrational to believe that anyone can anticipate every need of a project or program before it begins. Trying to be exact about every aspect of the outsourcing ensures that some part of the proposal will be wrong. The only outcome possible when mistakes become evident is renegotiation of the contract (expensive), acceptance of the wrong service (expensive), or screaming and shouting at each other (expensive).

The other type of RFP that creates problems is the vague RFP. These are written by organizations that believe that outsourcing means that 100 percent of the project will be done by the supplier, including the RFP, with little or no help from inside resources. As you read earlier, I do not believe that this is possible either.

In a vague RFP, the specifications are broad. They are often built quickly and with little thought. In a sense, the proposal must be created without a project definition—a situation which, as you now know, guarantees problems. Business and project objectives are not quantified, and measurements are nonexistent. These RFPs generally are used either to award contracts to suppliers who are picked before the RFP goes out or to outsource work that no purchaser really wants.

The implication of this type of RFP is that the supplier is trusted. Indeed, trust may exist at the beginning, but the lack of communication and the lack of a clear project definition ensures that performance will soon suffer. At that point, trust will degrade quickly, killing any initial benefit that came from early trust. Both parties will fall away from each other, pointing fingers.

The best approach is to strike a balance between detail and vagueness. The RFP you issue should clearly specify all the information needed for the define phase:

- Scope
- Initial business and project objectives

- Risk

- Constraints

- Alternatives.

The RFP also should specify a single internal contact for the suppliers to talk with as they develop their proposal. One of the most bizarre practices of outsourcing is that many companies limit or refuse communication with the suppliers while the proposals are being written. This may seem fair to all suppliers, but in fact, it just creates more distance between the suppliers and the customers, which carries over into the project work.

The chosen supplier, then, is responsible for the plan phase and will create a schedule with milestones for evaluation by the purchaser. A communication plan will ensure that as the project plan changes, both supplier and customer are equally aware of the changes and maintain a good level of trust. The supplier also owns the manage phase; however, issues and surprises are dealt with through open communication between all parties. As described below, both parties will work on the review phase together.

Clearly, outsourcing requires an ongoing, strong relationship based on trust. It is important to remember that both an internal person and the supplier must allocate time to maintaining the relationship.

Contractor Law

Some tax issues exist when outsourcing work. The IRS criteria for determining whether someone should be treated as an external contractor or as an employee has been applied inconsistently. You may be found liable for back taxes and penalties as a company if you treat an external contractor as an employee. Here are some of the criteria used by the IRS to determine whether a person should be treated as an external contractor or as an employee.

According to IRS guidelines, the criteria used for determining whether a contractor is being treated as an employee include the amount of instruction required, who pays for the training, the integration of the work, the services rendered, hiring, supervising and paying assistants, length of the relationship, hours of work and who sets them, work the contractor does for others, where the work is done, scheduling, status reporting, payment schedule, reimbursement of travel and business expenses, profit sharing, and right to terminate. Check with the IRS for the most up-to-date requirements, because the law is often challenged. Another good source is Tax Management Inc., a subsidiary of the Bureau of National Affairs.

This area of the law changes frequently and is difficult for a training person to monitor. Make sure that you involve your legal department with any contracting that you do, and proactively set up some time once a year to have a legal department or advisor evaluate your outsourcing plans.

Another useful resource is the Website www.WorkerStatus.com. This site has a wealth of information about court precedence, law changes, and guidelines. The following information comes from the WorkerStatus site:

> With regard to the [purchaser of services], the worker (service provider) must meet one of four criteria:
>
> - The first criteria [sic] is that the worker must have a place of business. Presumably, if a court reporter keeps an office at home, that would qualify as a "place of business."
> - The second criteria [sic] is that the worker must not primarily work in the recipient's facilities unless the worker pays a fair market rent for this use. In the rare situation where a court reporter has an office at the premises of the court reporting firm, the firm should be sure to collect a fair rent from the reporter. This is a good idea under the common-law rules as well as under this proposed law change.
> - The third criteria [sic] is that the worker operate "primarily from equipment not supplied by the service recipient." For the typical court reporter, this criteria [sic] is not a problem. Most court reporters use their own equipment.
> - The fourth criteria [sic] is that the worker not be required to work exclusively for the service recipient and have recently performed a significant amount of work for other persons, or have offered to perform services for persons through advertising, individual solicitations, listing with registries or other similar activities, or have worked under a registered or licensed business name. Often, a court reporter will become comfortable with one court reporting firm and not do much work for others. In this situation, meeting this element might be hard. Keep in mind that this is not currently the law and even if it becomes law, the firm needs to meet only one of the four criteria. Note that "listing with registries" satisfies this element. (James R. Urquhart III)

Confidentiality

Many companies require confidentiality agreements before they grant suppliers access to proprietary company information. Although you may be hiring someone to teach a workshop on something nonproprietary, the instructor will be in contact with people who may be working on sensitive projects. It is a good idea to be clear in advance that company information is not for public disclosure.

In addition, be careful what information you release in an RFP or in the discussion of an RFP with a prospective supplier. Although there is an element of lack of trust to this thought, it is vital to keep information about company information, rate information, and competitor information out of your discussions. Make sure that the people who will answer questions concerning the supplier contracts have been coached by your legal advisors on what can and cannot be said. Consider these seemingly innocuous questions that generally should not be answered:

- "Who else was sent a request for bid?" (Telling suppliers about their competitors can encourage them to practice a little corporate espionage, which is unethical, and can unfairly penalize anyone who did not ask.)

- "What price are you willing to pay?" (Starting with price, unless it is a constraint, will limit the creativity of the proposals and, again, may give the person who asked an unfair advantage.)

- "How far off were we compared with the person who got the contract?" (Although this question can be asked to get a better understanding of the market dynamics, it can set off lawsuits by suppliers who feel they have been eliminated unfairly.)

- "Who will make the final buy decision?" (Unless you plan to let the supplier talk with this person, don't tell. Fairness dictates that all suppliers speak to the same internal contact people.)

Establishing Communication Standards

Figure 8.3 depicts a scope diagram for a project designed to create a training registration system. You can use a scope diagram from the define phase to document which pieces will be done internally and which pieces will be done externally as a building block to the communication plan (see figure 8.3).

The stakeholder communication plan that you read about in the plan phase (chapter 3) is even more essential when work has been outsourced. If you are outsourcing components of the project, you should expand this

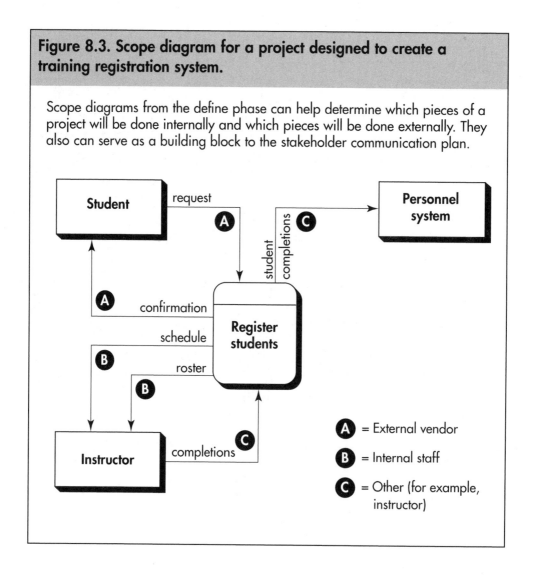

Figure 8.3. Scope diagram for a project designed to create a training registration system.

Scope diagrams from the define phase can help determine which pieces of a project will be done internally and which pieces will be done externally. They also can serve as a building block to the stakeholder communication plan.

plan to include communication with the supplier. For each major deliverable, there needs to be one supplier "owner" and one internal "owner"—that is, a single point of contact with the responsibility and authority for the decisions that need to be made. As figure 8.4 shows, each owner can have more than one deliverable; if it is possible, having one "overall owner" for the supplier and internal organization is useful as well.

Figure 8.5 depicts a relationship model that was popular during reengineering work in the mid-1980s. This type of model is a nice way to graphically display the internal and external roles on the project and how they will interface with each other; it also can clearly show whether a block or con-

Figure 8.4. Sample list of deliverables detailing who is responsible for each item.

For each major deliverable, there needs to be one supplier "owner" and one internal "owner" (see figure 8.5).

Company Contact	Supplier Contact	Required to Begin Work	Deliverables/Due Date
Internal B (555) 555-1212	Owner C (111) 555-1212	System parameters	Installed software Due: 5/1
Internal B	Owner A (222) 555-1212	Physical layout, volume, equipment	LAN Due: 5/15
Internal B	Owner A (222) 555-1212	Physical layout	Cabling Due: 5/30
Internal B	Owner E (333) 555-1212	Hardware specifications	Equipment Due: 6/15

straint exists in which one person is doing too much and everyone else is waiting on him or her.

Change Management

"I like long walks, especially when they are taken by people who annoy me." This quote attributed to Noel Coward nicely describes how many internal managers feel about their suppliers as projects hit inevitable snags. It is easiest in the short term to avoid conflict and change issues by hiding; it is the most damaging thing you can do in the long term.

Proactively, it is a great idea to set up a process for evaluating change as it occurs, because it will. The project plan, if not the project charter, is a great place in which to define this process. Here's a review of a sample change management process you read about in chapter 5:

Figure 8.5. A relationship model displaying the internal and external roles on a project and how they will interface with each other.

This type of model also can show whether a block or constraint exists in which one supplier is doing too much. For example, Supplier A has many interfaces with others and could be a roadblock.

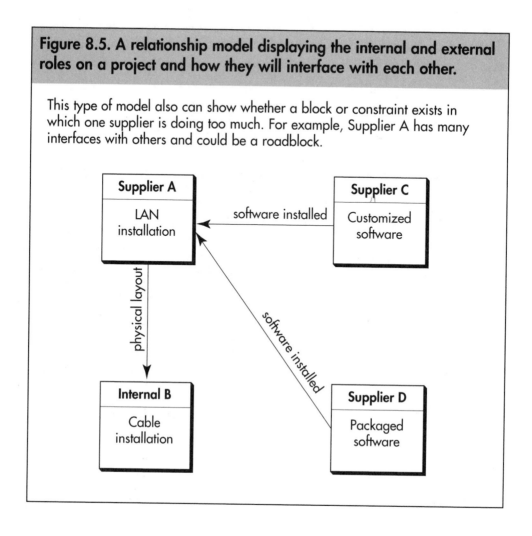

All changes to the scope, time, cost, or quality of the project will have to be documented and submitted to the pre-agreed key suppliers, internal contacts, and customers for rating. The rating, using a nautical theme, might be:

1. The boat has sunk, drop everything else.
2. The boat is taking on water, and will sink in the future.
3. The boat has a small leak, but can hobble along for awhile.

The people charged with coming up with the rating will come to a consensus:

• Make the change immediately.

• Make the change at a later date (specified).

• Delay the change.

Change can have a damaging effect on the progress of a project team, and adding a supplier to the mix magnifies most peoples' discomfort. Discomfort comes from the following elements:

- Self-interest: The stakeholders feel they will lose something of value.

- Misunderstanding or lack of trust: The stakeholders expect the worst.

- Different assessments: Different stakeholders have different cost-benefit perceptions.

- Low tolerance for change: Stakeholders fear they will not be able to change quickly enough.

Different strategies will be useful for different types of needs. Table 8.1 lists the advantages and disadvantages of different types of change initiatives. Planning for transition is usually part of the work that must be done internally—it is not a good place for outsourcing. Clear connection to a person in the organization is essential for change initiatives to take place and succeed at an individual level. For more thoughts about managing change and transition, I recommend the books by William Bridges (see resource list).

Before working with outside suppliers, sharpen your negotiating techniques. A good approach begins with the belief that the focus should be on the issue at hand and not the relationship. Do not confuse the two, and do not forget the importance of behaving with trust. The intent is to come up with a win-win solution. William Ury, in his book *Getting Past No* (New York: Bantam Books, 1991), shares the following five useful steps of negotiating

1. *Start with the outcome in mind.* If negotiations fail, what will you do to satisfy your interests without agreement? What are your interests, their interests, independent measuring standards? What's the least you'll take not to walk away? What is your best alternative to a negotiated agreement (BATNA)? What is their BATNA?

2. *Go to the balcony.* Imagine seeing the negotiation from above. When someone negotiates with you using tricks like false data, refusal to take ownership, stonewalling, attacks, or add-ons to muddy the water, remove yourself personally from the emotions. Don't get mad or get even. Know your hot buttons, use silence to buy time, rewind and rephrase to mirror what you've heard, or take a timeout.

3. *Step to their side.* Take their position by listening, acknowledging, agreeing (where you can), and showing respect. Do the unpredictable

Table 8.1. Advantages and Disadvantages of Different Types of Change Initiatives.

Approach	Situation	Advantages	Disadvantages
Education and communication	Lack of or inaccurate information and analysis	People will help with implementation	Is time consuming
Participation and involvement	Considerable power to resist	People have ownership	Is time consuming
Facilitation and support	Resistance because of adjustment problems	Is best for adjustment problems	Is time consuming
Negotiation and agreement	Some group clearly will lose out	Is an easy way to avoid major resistance	Is too expensive
Manipulation and trickery	Other tactics won't work or are too costly	Is quick and inexpensive	Holds future problems
Coercion	Speed is essential and the change agent has considerable power	Is speedy	Holds future payback

by accumulating "yeses"—"I can see why you feel that way" or "Yes, you make a good point."

4. *Reframe.* Move from concrete positions to more intangible issues. Accept their position, then redirect by saying "Tell me more" or "Help me understand what has put you in this stressful situation?" Brainstorm win-win solutions together.

5. *Build a bridge.* Use their values and interests to build the solution together and then create a way for the "opponent" to save face and have victory. As Sun Tzu said, "Build your opponent a golden bridge to retreat across."

Knowledge Transfer

Finally, be sure time is budgeted for the supplier and customer to share knowledge through the postproject review. Many contracts are set up to reward (through payment) only completed deliverables (for example, the delivery of a workshop) and do not include criteria for knowledge transfer to the internal staff. Time must be built into the contract and the project plan to determine the knowledge that must be transferred to internal staff, the way it will be transferred, and how the transfer will be measured for accountability of both parties. A great amount of valuable business knowledge walks out the door at the end of outsourced projects.

Shared Risk

Consider being specific up front about how the internal and external partners will share the risk of the outsourced project. In their book *The Discipline of Market Leaders* (Reading, MA, Perseus Press, 1997), Treacy and Wiersema introduce the term *customer intimacy.* Because outsourcing in the training field is almost always for the delivery of a service, it often makes sense to build a customer intimate relationship, meaning that both the provider and the purchaser of services equally share the cost of failure and the benefits of success. Consider what will happen in the following situations:

- The project deliverables are late. (Options: sliding pay scale, fines, penalties)
- The project deliverables are not high enough quality. (Options: predetermined quality measurements, escalation procedures)
- The project deliverables are over budget or too expensive. (Options: development of renegotiation guidelines at the start, padding)

Summary

In this chapter, you have read about how to manage outsourcing of training services. You have learned the importance of trust, contracting, contractor law, clear communication, management of change, and effective communication. To summarize, here are some pointers:

- Appoint an internal project leader with accountability for both internal and external personnel.

- Explain to your staff why and how the consultant or supplier will be used.

- Balance flexibility of requirements with need for control.

- Put your expectations in writing, including milestones. Hold regular performance reviews (before there is trouble).

- Measure consistently and choose measurements carefully.

- Check references of all workers carefully. Years of service do not guarantee they have the skills you need. Design a shared reward for both internal and external team members.

- Build contingency plans for all work.

- Don't let suppliers staff up too soon—if too many staff are around during the analysis phase, people will build before they analyze.

- Act as though you trust each other.

As in previous chapters, you now have the opportunity to apply what you have read to your own work.

Practical Exercises

Now practice creating an outsourcing plan. Again, think about your own project and consider some aspect of your project that could be outsourced. Go back and review the documents that you created during the define and plan phases for your own project, and determine what the ramifications would be to these documents. How would they change?

Exercise 8.1. Create a relationship matrix.

Thinking about your own project, create a relationship matrix detailing the interactions between supplier and internal staff (see figure 8.5 for an example). Write the name of each supplier and company department working on the project in a separate box. Draw lines between the boxes to show the necessary lines of communication.

Supplier name
Deliverable

Supplier name
Deliverable

Supplier name
Deliverable

Supplier name
Deliverable

Supplier name
Deliverable

Exercise 8.2. Create a list of deliverables.

For the component of your project that will be outsourced, create a list of deliverables detailing what will be expected from each supplier (see figure 8.4 for an example).

Company Contact	Supplier Contact	Required to Begin Work	Deliverables/Due Date

Chapter 9

The Project Begins . . .

Q: How can I get started managing my projects more effectively?

A: Create a checklist to jump-start your transition.

In this book, you have learned how to do the following:

- Determine the tasks that need to be done by the project manager and those that should be done by a developer

- Build a project charter to document business objectives, learning objectives, scope, risk, and constraints

- Build a project plan for new course development, course acquisition, or contracted training projects

- Create a work breakdown structure to uncover the activities needed to complete a project

- Plan and manage the cost of training projects

- Create critical path networks and bar charts to manage the project schedule and resource allocation

- Accurately estimate work effort for a project

- Perform a postproject review for every project to ensure the management of project intellectual capital.

Congratulations! You are on your way to managing your projects more effectively. Here is a fun exercise to emphasize that you *can* control the future (at least a little):

- Think of a number between two and nine.
- Multiply that number by nine.
- Add the two numbers together.
- Subtract five.
- Assign a letter to the number, using the formula 1 = A, 2 = B, 3 = C, and so forth. Think of a country that starts with the letter that goes with your number.
- Using the second letter of that country's name, think of a large animal whose name starts with that letter.
- Finally, think of the color that is usually associated with this large animal.

Are you thinking of a gray elephant from Denmark? Statistics tell us that there is a good chance that you will be thinking of those three words. First, the process forces you to end up with the number four if the math is done correctly, regardless of the number you start with. Apparently, Denmark is about the only country that begins with the letter D that people can think of easily, and elephants are the most common large animals that people think of, especially when restricted to the letter E. Finally, most people think that elephants are gray.

What you have experienced, both in this little exercise and in this book, is a process that encourages repeatable, predictable success. You will be faced with many different types of projects in your career, but The Dare Approach increases your chance of project success.

You might want to keep checklists for the define, plan, manage, and review stages handy—in your calendar, on your wall, or on your desk (see figure 9.1).

Figure 9.1. Sample checklists for the define, plan, manage, and review stages.

A Checklist for Define

Have you remembered to . . .

- ☐ Document the business objectives?
- ☐ Document the learning objectives?
- ☐ Document scope?
- ☐ Document risk?
- ☐ Document constraints?
- ☐ Create a stakeholder communication plan?

A Checklist for Plan

Have you remembered to . . .

- ☐ Finalize the business and learning objectives?
- ☐ Create a list of activities to schedule (optional: work breakdown structure)?
- ☐ Use a course development methodology to choose the right activities (such as *The Learner First Approach*)?
- ☐ Use a performance consulting methodology to choose the right activities (such as *The PACT Approach*)?
- ☐ Create the schedule (using the critical path method and Gantt charts)?
- ☐ Work back from the fixed date if necessary?
- ☐ Estimate activity durations?
- ☐ Plan for milestones and review?
- ☐ Choose and apply project management software?
- ☐ Create the budget?

(continued next page)

Figure 9.1. *(continued)*

A Checklist for Manage

Have you remembered to . . .

☐ Establish monitoring criteria using risk assessment, constraints, scenarios, the schedule, and the budget worksheet created during the define phase?

☐ Create and implement a plan to manage changing constraints and requirements?

☐ Create a strategy for troubleshooting changing constraints and requirements?

☐ Prepare a strategy for contracting outsourced work?

☐ Prepare a strategy for managing and controlling outsourced work?

A Checklist for Review

Have you remembered to . . .

☐ Individually review the project using a postproject review template?

☐ Review the project as a team using a postproject review template?

☐ Perform detailed analysis of a project using systems thinking?

Summary

To conclude, go forward into your project work with courage. Realize with certainty that surprise and change are key components of project work. Also realize with certainty that you are a brilliant, experienced professional with new tools to remain flexible yet focused. I leave you with this little story from the Internet to illustrate that strange things happen to all projects, but if you "dare to properly manage resources" and proceed with integrity and a flexible structure, everything works out in the end.

After initiating an SOS, a Japanese fishing trawler's crew was rescued at sea. When asked what happened to their boat, they replied that it had been destroyed by a flying cow. Since this was a pretty ridiculous claim, they were put in jail.

Later, a Russian aircrew confessed that one of them had stolen a cow and smuggled it on to their plane. When the plane took off, the cow panicked and started charging around. The crew, in order to save the plane, pushed the cow out the door into (they thought) the sea. It turns out that it landed on and sank the Japanese trawler. The Japanese fishermen were vindicated.

Resources

Andrews, A., Dorine C., and Stalick, S. *Business Reengineering—The Survival Guide.* Englewood Cliffs, NJ: Prentice Hall, 1994.

Archibald, R.D. *Managing High-Technology Programs & Projects,* 2nd Edition. New York: John Wiley & Sons, 1998.

Armstrong, T. *In Their Own Way.* Los Angeles: Jeremy P. Tarcher, 1987.

Armstrong, T. *7 Kinds of Smart: Identifying & Developing Your Many Intelligences.* New York: Penguin Books, 1993.

Baggerman, L. "The Futility of Downsizing." *Industry Week,* January 18, 1993.

Boddie, J. *Crunch Mode: Building Effective Systems on a Tight Schedule.* New York: Yourdon Press, 1987.

Bridges, W. *Managing Transitions: Making the Most of Change.* Reading, MA: Addison-Wesley, 1991.

Brooks, F. *The Mythical Man Month.* Reading, MA: Addison-Wesley, 1975.

Champy, J., and Hammer, M. *Reengineering the Corporation.* New York: HarperCollins, 1993.

Chang, R.Y. *Success Through Teamwork.* San Diego, CA: Pfeiffer and Co., 1994.

Davenport, T. "Managing Information in a Process Context." Chicago: Ernst & Young Center for Information Technology and Strategy, Working paper 13, April 1992.

Davenport, T. *Process Innovation: Reengineering Work Through Information Technology.* Boston: Harvard Business School Press, 1992.

Davenport, T., and Prusak, L. *Working Knowledge: How Organizations Manage What They Know.* Boston: Harvard Business School Press, 1997.

De Bono, E. *Six Thinking Hats.* New York: MICA Management Resources, 1985.

DeMarco, T., and Lister, T. *Peopleware: Productive Projects and Teams,* 2nd Edition. New York: Dorset House, 1999.

Edwards, B. *Drawing on the Right Side of the Brain.* New York: St. Martin's Press, 1988.

Ernst, R. *RealTime Coaching: How to Make the Minute by Minute Decisions That Unleash the Power in Your People.* Carmel, IN: Leadership Horizons, 1999.

Florida, R. *Rebuilding America: Lessons from the Heartland.* Pittsburgh, PA: Carnegie Mellon University, 1992.

Frost P., Mitchell, V., and Nord, W. *Organizational Reality Reports from the Firing Line.* Glenview, IL: Scott, Foresman, and Co., 1986.

Gardner, H. "Are There Additional Intelligences? The Case for Naturalist, Spiritual, and Existential Intelligences." White paper, Cambridge, MA: Harvard Graduate School of Education, 1996.

Gardner, H. *Frames of Mind.* New York: Basic Books, 1985.

Gardner, H. *Multiple Intelligences: The Theory in Practice.* New York: HarperCollins, 1993.

Gardner, H. *Intelligence Reframed: Multiple Intelligence for the 21st Century.* New York: Basic Books, 1999.

Gause, D., and Weinberg, G. *Exploring Requirements: Quality Before Design.* New York: Dorset House, 1989.

Greenleaf, R. *On Becoming a Servant Leader.* San Francisco: Jossey-Bass, 1996.

Hampton, D., Summer, C., and Webber, R. *Organizational Behavior and the Practice of Management.* Glenview, IL: Scott, Foresman, and Co., 1987.

Haynes, M.E. *Project Management.* Menlo Park, CA: Crisp Publications, 1989.

Highsmith, J.A. III. *Adaptive Software Development: An Evolutionary Approach to Managing Chaotic Projects.* New York: Dorset House, 1998.

Horwitz, J., and Kimpel, H. "Taking Control: Techniques Does the Group Interview." *Training & Development,* October 1988.

Hunt, V. Daniel. *Reengineering: Leveraging the Power of Integrated Product Development.* New York: John Wiley & Sons, 1995.

Johansson, H., McHugh, P., Pendlebury, A., Johansson, H., and Wheeler, W. *Business Process Reengineering: Breakpoint Strategies for Market Dominance.* New York: John Wiley & Sons, 1993.

Kahn, L. "The Art of the Interview." *Whole Earth Review,* Winter 1987.

Karten, N. *Managing Expectations.* New York: Dorset House, 1994.

Kerzner, H.D. *Project Management Workbook: A Systems Approach to Planning, Scheduling, and Controlling.* New York: Van Nostrand Reinhold, 1997.

Kirkpatrick, D. *Evaluating Training Programs: The Four Levels.* San Francisco: Berrett-Koehler, 1998.

Laborde, G. *Influencing with Integrity.* Palo Alto, CA: Syntony Publishing, 1984.

Lewis, J.P. *Fundamentals of Project Management.* New York: AMACOM, 1995.

Margulies, N. *Mapping Inner Space: Learning and Teaching Mind Mapping.* Tucson, AZ: Zephyr Press, 1991.

Michalko, M. *Thinkertoys.* Berkeley, CA: Ten Speed Press, 1991.

Morris, D., and Brandon, J. *Reengineering Your Business.* New York: McGraw-Hill, 1993.

Nonaka, I., Takeuchi, H., and Takeuchi, H. *The Knowledge-Creating Company: How Japanese Companies Create the Dynamics of Innovation.* New York: Oxford University Press, 1995.

Penner, D. *The Project Manager's Survival Guide.* Columbus, OH: Battelle Press, 1994.

Rakos, J.J. *Software Project Management for Small to Medium Sized Projects.* Upper Saddle River, NJ: Prentice Hall, 1990.

Roberts, W. *Leadership Secrets of Attila the Hun.* New York: Warner Books, 1987.

Robinson, D., and Robinson, J. *Performance Consulting: Moving Beyond Training.* San Francisco: Berrett-Koehler, 1996.

Rummler, G., and Brache, A. *Improving Performance: How to Manage the White Space on the Organizational Chart.* San Francisco: Jossey-Bass, 1995.

Russell, L. *The Accelerated Learning Fieldbook: Making the Instructional Process Fast, Flexible, and Fun.* San Francisco: Jossey-Bass Pfeiffer, 1999.

Senge, P.M. *The Fifth Discipline: The Art & Practice of the Learning Organization.* New York: Doubleday, 1990.

Senge, P.M., Kleiner, A., and Roberts, C. *The Fifth Discipline Fieldbook: Strategies and Tools for Building a Learning Organization.* New York: Doubleday, 1994.

"Special Supplement on Reengineering." *Information Week,* May 10, 1993.

Thomsett, R. *People and Project Management.* New York: Yourdon Press, 1980.

Treacy, M., and Wiersema, F. *The Discipline of Market Leaders.* Reading, MA: Perseus Press, 1997.

Ury, W. *Getting Past No: Negotiating Your Way from Confrontation to Cooperation.* New York: Bantam Books, 1991.

van der Heijden, K. *Scenarios: The Art of Strategic Conversation.* New York: John Wiley & Sons, 1996.

Weinberg, G. *Quality Software Management, Vol. 3, Congruent Action.* New York: Dorset House, 1994.

Wheatley, M. *Leadership and the New Science.* San Francisco: Berrett-Koehler, 1994.

Whyte, D. *The Heart Aroused: Poetry and the Preservation of the Soul in Corporate America.* New York: Doubleday, 1996.

Websites

Note: The online references are from the World Wide Web and include the appropriate URL address. Please keep in mind that in the future, some of these sites might move or be discontinued.

Information on Contractor Law

Bureau of National Affairs; www.bnatax.com

James R. Urquhart III; www.WorkerStatus.com

Information on Project Management

American Society for Training & Development; www.astd.org

Georgia Tech Research Institute (multimedia development tools); www.mime1.marc.gatech.edu/tim/mm_tools/default.htm

International Alliance for Learning; www.ialearn.org

The International Project Management Association; www.ipma.ch

International Project Management Help Desk; www.geocities.com/Athens/Delphi/8390

International Society for Performance Improvement; www.ispi.org

Michael J. Collins, The Training Professional's Gateway;
    homepage.eircom.net/~mjcollins

The Project Management Boulevard (Web resources); www.pmblvd.com

The Project Management Center; www. infogoal.com/pmc/pmchome.htm

Project Management Forum; www.pmforum.org

Project Management Institute; www.pmi.org

Society for Human Resource Development; www.shrm.org

Synapse (a directory of project management resources); www.synapse.net

Training Forum (gateway for training resources); www.trainingforum.com

Newsletters

The Independent Contractor Report
    James R. Urquhart III, publisher
    A Professional Law Corporation
    15181 Nantes Circle
    Irvine, CA 92604

Thiagi Game Letter
    Sivasailam Thiagarajan, author
    Jossey-Bass Pfeiffer Publishers
    www.jbp.com

Lou Russell president and CEO of Russell Martin & Associates, a consulting and training company focusing on improving planning, process, and performance. She has served as a consultant to companies, schools, churches, and colleges to help them expand their organizational ability to learn. She is the author of *The Accelerated Learning Fieldbook, Project Management for Trainers*, and *IT Leardership Alchemy*. She can be reached via email at info@russellmartin.com.